Cheated On

The Divorce Minister Guide for Surviving Infidelity and Keeping Your Faith

By Rev. David Derksen

Copyright © 2018 David Derksen

All rights reserved. This book or parts thereof may not be reproduced in any form, stored in any retrieval system, or transmitted in any form by any means—electronic, mechanical, photocopy, recording, or otherwise—without prior written permission of the publisher, except as provided by the United States of America copyright law. For permission requests, write to the publisher—at "Attention: Permissions Coordinator"—at the address below:

Divorce Minister
Minneapolis-St. Paul, MN
info@divorceminister.com
www.divorceminister.com
Printed in the United States of America
First Printing, 2018
ISBN: 978-1-7329541-0-6 (eBook)
ISBN: 978-1-7329541-1-3 (paperback)

Other Copyright Notices:

This book is written and published to provide accurate and authoritative information relevant to the subject matter presented. The author and publisher believe all the statements made in this book are true. This work is published and sold with the understanding that the author and publisher are not engaged in rendering legal, medical, or mental health professional services by reason of their authorship or publication of this book. If medical, legal, mental health, or other expert assistance is required, the services of a competent professional person should be sought.

Scripture quotations marked by NIV are from THE HOLY BIBLE, NEW INTERNATIONAL VERSION®, NIV® Copyright © 1973, 1978, 1984, 2011 by Biblica, Inc.® Used by permission. All rights reserved worldwide.

Scripture quotations marked NLT are taken from the Holy Bible, New Living Translation, copyright © 1996, 2004, 2007 by Tyndale House Foundation. Used by permission of Tyndale House Publishers, Inc., Carol Stream, Illinois 60188. All rights reserved.

Scripture quotations marked with NKJV taken from the New King James Version®. Copyright © 1982 by Thomas Nelson. Used by permission. All rights reserved.

Scripture quotations marked with NASB taken from the NEW AMERICAN STANDARD BIBLE®, Copyright © 1960, 1962, 1963, 1968, 1971, 1972, 1973, 1975, 1977, 1995 by The Lockman Foundation. Used by permission.

Scripture quotations marked with NRSV are from the New Revised Standard Version Bible, copyright © 1989 the Division of Christian Education of the National Council of the Churches of Christ in the United States of America. Used by permission. All rights reserved.

Scripture quotations marked TPT are from The Passion Translation®. Copyright © 2017, 2018 by Passion & Fire Ministries, Inc. Used by permission. All rights reserved. ThePassionTranslation.com.

Scripture quotations marked with (KJV) taken from the King James Version. Public Domain.

Acknowledgments

Allen and Char Derksen. My parents are a major reason this book exists. In addition to being pillars of love for me during my darkest days, they both have helped tremendously to financially launch this project. Their unwavering faith in me and what God is doing through me are precious gifts for which I am truly grateful.

Aubree. God turned my ashes into beauty when He brought Aubree into my life. I could never guess married life could be so fun and full of joy as it has been these past years with Aubree as my wife. She brought laughter back into the halls of my soul. Thank you, sweetheart, for all your support as I launched *Divorce Minister: Taking Adultery Seriously* and transformed those ideas into this book!

Naolin. My munchkin. You are the joy of this father's heart. I cannot believe God would be so extravagant as to grant me the privilege of raising such an amazing and spunky little girl.

Chump Lady, Tracy Schorn. I can only begin to thank you for blazing a path for this book and encouraging me along the way. Your insights into the publishing process have been invaluable. Thank you so very much for everything!

Dee Parsons of The Wartburg Watch. Your support and all you do with Deb to expose spiritual abuse in the church world is an inspiration! Thank you for your encouragement and help as I worked on making this book a reality.

Christopher Trimble. Thank you for your hard work in both designing the book cover and formatting the manuscript for publication. I have thoroughly enjoyed working with you in launching this book project. Thank you for all your patience as I settled on just the right cover, style, and wording!

Kerri Miller. Thank you for all you have done to help whip this manuscript into shape! I appreciate all the encouragement as well as your skill at helping me produce a manuscript worthy of publication. It has been a delight working with you.

Thank you to my colleagues and friends who have helped me shape this project. Rev. Chris Wheatley, Rev. Jon Ungerland, Rev. Pete Sherry, and all those friends via the blog and Facebook who gave me such quality feedback. Thank you!

Most importantly, this book would not exist apart from my Jesus loving and rescuing me from the deep pit of despair that came when I discovered my first wife was cheating on and leaving me. I am convinced He sent his angels and His true followers to remind me of His great love for me, which gave me hope.

Thank you, Jesus, for sending your "ravens" as you sent them to minister to the prophet Elijah (I Kings 17:2-6). I am proud to call you my Lord, my savior, and my truest friend.

I hope all who read these pages will discover a new or deeper appreciation of you, Jesus, as such a wonderful and faithful friend!

Contents

Acknowledgments ....

Introduction 1

   A Divorce Minister Welcome 1

The Basics

Chapter 1 - Spiritual Realities Regarding Adultery...............................6

Chapter 2 – The Shared Responsibility Lie...13

Chapter 3 - A Godly Divorce 19

Troublesome Texts

Chapter 4 - Malachi 2:16—But God Hates Divorce! 27

Chapter 5 - Book of Hosea—Marriage Advice, Really?........................31

Chapter 6 - Ephesians 5:21-33—Blame-Shifting at its "Finest" 37

Confounding Concepts

Chapter 7 - Grief as Primary 41

Chapter 8 - Godly Forgiveness 47

Chapter 9 - Righteous Restoration And Reconciliation.........................57

Other Considerations

Chapter 10 - The Kids..71

Chapter 11 - Abandonment, Abuse, And Annulment 77

Chapter 12 - False Friends & Ex In-Laws 87

Chapter 13 - Is It Really "Just" An Emotional Affair? 93

Conclusion - Testifying To Real Hope..99

About The Author 103

Introduction
A Divorce Minister Welcome

"All praise to God, the Father of our Lord Jesus Christ. God is our merciful Father and the source of all comfort. He comforts us in all our troubles so that we can comfort others. When they are troubled, we will be able to give them the same comfort God has given us."
– 2 Corinthians 1:3-4, NLT

"I Was Cheated On."

This statement is true for me. I was cheated on by my first wife, and the marriage ended in divorce.

If you are reading these words, I suspect you were somehow touched by the trauma of infidelity as well. This book is for you.

I wrote this book to speak life and encouragement to the faithful party. This is not another *why-haven't-you-forgiven-them-already*, beat-down book from a pastor.

You see, this book is my attempt to share a pastor's perspective I knew I needed as I went through my own trauma-filled journey through adultery discovery and divorce.

My hope is this book will communicate to you, dear faithful spouse, a love from God that will help you hold onto your faith.

I do not say that lightly. I know this is no easy task as your Christian faith likely was weaponized against you in this awful time.

You have experienced enough losses. The loss of a relationship with your loving God need not be another one.

While I say this is a pastoral guide, I want to be clear this book comes with some very strong messages. Some may even accuse me of anger and condemnation for writing these things.

I am okay with such accusations.

Abuse and evil make God angry. I have no problem condemning both abuse and evil. In my "angry," passionate words, I hope you hear and feel God's love for the victim and passion to protect the abused.

Make no mistake:

Marital infidelity is incredibly abusive! Plus, God calls adultery evil (see Deuteronomy 22:22) and has anger toward the wicked all the time (see Psalm 7:11).

Because I so strongly oppose abuse and evil, I take what some may consider a "divorce-positive" stance.

This may be one of the most divorce-positive books you will ever read from an evangelical minister.

I have no problem advocating for divorce under the circumstances this book addresses. Divorce is not the greatest evil nor even the greatest threat to godly Christian marriages or godly families. The Christian community has been sold a lie to think otherwise.

Does this mean I recommend divorce for all marriage problems?

No.

I *do* believe divorce can be a sin if done simply to marry another, such as a cheating husband chasing after his "beloved" mistress, or a promiscuous wife rushing after the sexual attention of her extramarital "sugar daddy."

That said, some spiritual circumstances call for divorce, just as some circumstances call for amputation in the medical world.

It would be preferable never to enter into a situation where such an amputation is necessary. But we do not live in a perfect world.

To be clear:

1. I am not selling magical thinking "forgiveness" steps (as if all the faithful party needs to do is "forgive" and all is well).
2. I am not selling steps to "affair-proof" your marriage.
3. I am not selling false hope in reconciliation with an unrepentant cheater.
4. I am not selling any excuses or justifications (as if they exist!) for cheating on a spouse.

This book is about cutting through the confusion regarding cheating within the Christian community.

It is not a book about "saving" infidelity-ravaged marriages, although some marriages might be rebuilt and restored due to the hard-hitting, biblical perspective I share here.

That said, this book is for those who have experience being cheated on. I am writing this as your pastoral champion.

Sometimes that means wielding my pastoral "staff" to beat back wolves trying to tear into the sheep who are dear to my heart. Wolves wearing sheep's clothes are plentiful in these situations.

The words in this book are not gentle to those in that crowd. They are blunt and might "bite." I make no apology for that.

I refuse to tolerate further abuse of faithful spouses.

If you are looking for a book that "sees both sides," then I suggest that you pick up one of the plentiful, psycho-babble books from the self-help shelves.

Abuse and evil are never justified. You do not have to understand the "other side" to know that the abuse and evil need to stop.

Rev. David Derksen

Another warning:
The subject matter of this book is dark.

Adultery, emotional affairs, abandonment, and divorce are not generally seen as "light conversation." I understand this.

However, people are dying emotionally and spiritually because of the pastoral reluctance to talk plainly about the evils inherent in such situations.

Satan and his minions are thriving in the darkness we pastors cede to him by refusing to acknowledge such evil exists, and he operates in our churches, communities, and even among the people we dearly love.

Digging into the subject matter of infidelity means digging into the deep dung of human depravity.

It is stinky, squishy, and can make one feel fouled by the mere thought of it. *But we must grit our teeth and push through the discomfort.*

Why?

We cannot help someone in such a pit unless we ourselves are willing to get dirty with them. Many victims of infidelity need great help after finding themselves flung into that pit by a conniving, cheating spouse.

This book aims to give those victims of infidelity—i.e., the faithful spouses—a helping hand out of that stinking pit. Plus, my hope is this book can help other pastors and Christian leaders provide faithful spouses more reliable and godly support in the dark times that come after discovering infidelity.

Another important piece to note is my perspective. I write this book as a professional chaplain—a Board Certified Chaplain (BCC)— and an ordained evangelical minister.

Besides my years of experience working with faithful spouses via my blog and my own personal experience of surviving divorce after the adulterous betrayal of my first wife, I draw heavily upon the Bible as the authoritative source on handling divorce, infidelity, abandonment, and annulment.

This is not a secular guidebook but a guidebook designed for people struggling to make sense of infidelity in light of God's will and guidance. My hope is this book will help faithful spouses retain their Christian faith despite experiencing such human depravity firsthand.

This book is a pastoral resource grounded deeply and firmly within the Christian tradition.

I write as a pastor and adultery-survivor who is unashamed of my commitment to God, the Bible, and the Gospel. In fact, a significant portion of this book utilizes the Bible to support faithful spouses while also correcting some of the most egregious textual abuses on this subject matter.

This is not a Bible commentary or an exegetical treatise.

I am not a biblical scholar providing in-depth textual criticism for each related biblical passage on the topics of infidelity and divorce. *That is not the aim of my work.*

Plenty of excellent resources exist out there tackling the minutiae of the original languages and the historical context of such passages. Another book doing just that is not needed today.

What is needed is a book providing a practical theology on matters relating to infidelity and divorce.

This is a book geared to provide real-time spiritual and emotional support to those in the pit of an infidelity-ravaged marriage. We begin by unpacking what adultery is in the eyes of God

Chapter 1
Spiritual Realities
Regarding Adultery

"Do you not know that your bodies are members of Christ himself? Shall I then take the members of Christ and unite them with a prostitute? Never! Do you not know that he who unites himself with a prostitute is one with her in body? For it is said, 'The two will become one flesh.' But whoever is united with the Lord is one with him in spirit."
– 1 Corinthians 6:15-17, NIV

Adultery is soul rape.

This is the bitter truth we learn from Apostle Paul's first letter to the Corinthians. When a spouse unites with another man or woman in a sexual act, that spouse is also uniting this third party to the faithful spouse *against his or her expressed wishes.*

It is rape.

The oneness of soul and spirit is invaded by a third party (or more). This spiritual truth explains why adultery is such a traumatic experience for the faithful spouse.

Adultery means the faithful spouse's very soul was violated and the oneness of the marriage defiled through the cheating spouse uniting with another.

The experience of discovering that our spouse cheated leaves permanent marks. That moment is forever etched in the faithful one's mind in technicolor replete with all the smells and sounds, as if time has frozen.

It is a sucker-punch from Hell. The pain is searing and deep, very deep. It is a soul-level trauma. The violation goes to our core.

This spiritual truth–adultery is soul rape–also helps illustrate why so many so-called Christian responses to faithful spouses are so wrong.

I hope everyone reading this understands why asking a rape victim for his or her part in being raped is highly inappropriate and ungodly.

The same thing applies here.

It is heartless and ungodly to ask the victim of soul rape to share what part they played in "asking for" this heinous violation of their marriage and very soul.

Whatever you may have been told or taught, a faithful spouse did not ask to be soul raped!

Another important lesson this spiritual truth can teach us is about the lasting impact such an experience has on soul rape victims. Adulterous betrayal is a deep spiritual and emotional trauma that needs to be treated as such.

With the discovery of infidelity, the faithful spouse's world has been blown up by the cheater. The faithful spouse is left wondering what is true and who can be trusted after such an intimate and humiliating betrayal by his or her spouse.

It will take time to grieve such catastrophic losses and heal such deep wounds.

Rape survivors carry lasting emotional and spiritual scars from their horrifying experience. Telling a victim to just "get over it" or "don't talk about it" is far from kind or loving.

In the same way, soul rape survivors need safe space to grieve and heal. Faithful spouses need people to listen to them without condemnation.

Telling a soul rape survivor to "get over it" or "don't talk about it" only compounds the devastating rejection from their spouse.

Please extend the same compassion, patience, and gentleness to faithful spouses that you would to a rape victim trying to recover from her trauma.

If you cannot handle listening to their story, own that for yourself. Let the faithful spouse know that the problem is you and not them.

Whatever you do, please do not shame the faithful spouse for needing to share their story in their effort to grieve and heal from soul rape.

Like discarded, used tissue paper.

As a soul rape survivor, a faithful spouse may feel an acute sense of shame. Adulterous betrayal comes with a profound sense of violation and rejection.

I will never forget hearing a pastor describe her feelings the morning after surviving a sexual assault. She felt like "used tissue paper."

Those words are powerful expressions of how a soul rape victim feels, especially when the revelation is fresh.

This shame is why I refer to spouses as faithful spouses as opposed to adultery victims. I choose to focus on our virtue and value as opposed to what was done to us.

We have value. We are virtuous. We have integrity. We stayed faithful.

Faithful spouses need to hear these truths. The shame needs to be beaten back by friends and fellow Christians reminding them of how God values and loves them.

"For our struggle is not against flesh and blood, but against the rulers, against the authorities, against the powers of this dark world and against the spiritual forces of evil in the heavenly realms."
– Ephesians 6:12, NIV

Besides understanding adultery as soul rape, it is important to recognize that these situations have a spiritual warfare component.

If you have ever talked with more than one survivor of infidelity or read the literature describing cheaters' excuses, you will soon discover the lies cheaters tell are common and unoriginal.

It is as if they were all given:

THE POOR CAUGHT-CHEATER'S BOOK OF EXCUSES.

Here are some of the old standbys in this cheater's handbook:

- *"You drove me to cheat by your _____ [weight gain, overworking, frigidity, lack of attention...insert use of tailor-made grievance here]."*

- *"We were already divorced in our hearts."*

- *"I needed to repent of making our marriage an idol."*

- *"God would want me to be happy."*

- *"Our marriage was always just a lie."*

- *"God is calling me to sacrifice our marriage as He called Abraham to sacrifice Isaac, his son."*

What strikes me when I read Christian literature on the subject of marital infidelity is that none I've found actually identifies a biblical explanation for the coordination of cheater lies and abuse of faithful spouses.

For a serious student of Scripture, the explanation is obvious:

It is demonic.

Scripture is very clear that Satan is the author of lies (see John 8:44). It is his nature. Furthermore, we know that Satan makes plans or schemes to destroy us (see 2 Corinthians 2:10-11, 1 Peter 5:8).

So, what can we conclude about the origin of a situation that is marked by a common set of coordinated lies designed to destroy lives and marriages?

It is pretty obvious:

Satan and his demonic minions are involved.

This does NOT mean the cheater is absolved for his or her choice to commit adultery! "The Devil made me do it" will not cut it on Judgment Day. Nor should such an excuse ever cut it in any biblical pastor's office.

The adultery and accompanying lies are one hundred percent on the cheater.

They opened the door and welcomed the demons in with open arms. Now they are dining with them.

The only way out is through repentance and asking God to purify their heart of all unrighteousness—more on that later. In fact, the cheater may even need the ministry of deliverance.

> "If a man is found sleeping with another man's wife, both the man who slept with her and the woman must die. You must purge the evil from Israel."
> – Deuteronomy 22:22, NIV

Besides recognizing that adultery is soul rape and that situations involving marital infidelity are true spiritual war zones, the last basic piece of orientation is to realize that marital infidelity impacts the whole community. It is not just "a private matter" between spouses (and the third party).

What continues to amaze me as a pastor and infidelity survivor is how Christians seem to lose their minds and fail to retain even a modicum of common sense when it comes to adultery.

> "It's a private matter," says a Christian who is unwilling to face the ugly, adulterous truth.

Really?! Like that whole marriage ceremony in front of the crowded church where the couple pledged lifelong fidelity?

How come that pledge is public and the breaking of it is suddenly "private"?

At minimum, a duly licensed third party was involved; otherwise, the marriage would not be considered valid in the eyes of the state.

You cannot get married or divorced without engaging the community in some way.

Similarly, God understands marriage and its violation as a matter impacting the whole community. Deuteronomy 22:22 clearly treats adultery as impacting the whole nation of Israel.

Anyone who has had friends whose marriage was impacted by infidelity understands this basic truth. The infidelity impacts everyone's relationship with this couple one way or another.

And this is true whether or not the couple is being open about the matter. *Trust me.*

Fair or not, your relationship with the faithful spouse is being assessed by this person as either safe or dangerous after such a deep betrayal by their spouse. And the cheater may be looking to you for cover in "justifying" or hiding their treacherous, sinful behavior.

Adultery is far from a "private matter." To treat it as such is dangerously naïve. The truth is that adultery impacts the entire community, and this truth has been known since the Old Testament was written.

Adultery is soul rape. Such situations are rife with spiritual warfare as evidenced by the common lies cheaters spout once caught, as well as the utterly destructive nature of the sin.

Adultery is not a private matter. It is destructive for the whole community, and the Bible is clear that it ought to be treated seriously as a community problem (see also Hebrews 13:4).

With these basic spiritual truths understood about adultery, we now turn to the most pernicious and prevalent lie about adultery promoted in the world and—sadly—among Christians:

The Shared Responsibility Lie.

Chapter 2
The Shared Responsibility Lie

> "This, then, is the law of jealousy when a woman goes astray and makes herself impure while married to her husband, or when feelings of jealousy come over a man because he suspects his wife. The priest is to have her stand before the LORD and is to apply this entire law to her. The husband will be innocent of any wrongdoing, but the woman will bear the consequences of her sin."
> – Numbers 5:29-31, NIV

These verses come from an obscure passage in Numbers. In this passage, a ritual is prescribed for dealing with suspected adultery in a wife.

The result of this ritual—if the wife was guilty of adultery—was either barrenness (a grave curse in Jewish culture as women were valued for the children they produced) or outright death, as some may read the physical curse mentioned in the passage. Either way, the sin of adultery was taken very seriously and punished severely under the Law of Moses.

I should emphasize that execution is not my suggestion. *I am not advocating for the return of the death penalty for cheaters.*

Punishment of adultery is not the point of this chapter or book for that matter. Rather, I want to highlight how God assigns guilt or blame for adultery, as it stands in stark contrast to how Christians too often do this.

A popular approach to handling adultery—even in evangelical churches (as I and others have experienced)—is to treat the adultery as a result of two people's choices. I call this "The Shared Responsibility Lie."

Sadly, Satan has been very busy selling this one with great success. Let me be crystal clear:

It is a lie.

Notice the last part of the passage from Numbers:

> "The husband will be **innocent** of any wrongdoing, but the woman will **bear the consequences** of her sin."
> – Numbers 5:31, NIV, emphasis added

This is a test for suspected adultery.

What part of the guilt for adultery or suspected adultery does the husband (faithful spouse) bear?

None.

Zero percent.

The faithful husband is assigned absolutely zero blame for the infidelity of his wife. Or to quote the Bible, the husband is "innocent of *any* wrongdoing" to be precise (emphasis mine).

Notice what this passage does NOT teach:

God does NOT say the priest needs to check to see if the husband was ignoring his wife's "emotional needs" and whether that caused her to commit adultery.

God does NOT ask whether the faithful party took too many business trips. Work responsibilities do not excuse the wife for committing adultery.

God does NOT say the priest needs to weigh the husband to see if he "let himself go" and ask whether the wife lost sexual interest in him, resulting in her "needing" to go elsewhere. This is not about the physical appearance of the faithful spouse.

God does NOT say the priest needs to assess bank accounts and work history of the husband to see if he is worthy of remaining married. This is not about the wealth of the faithful spouse.

God does NOT say to question the wife to see if she was "unhappy" in her marriage and needed some excitement. This is not a report card on the faithful spouse's ability to make his wife happy.

When the question is about adultery, the focus is upon the spouse who chose to sin.

I would assert this is also true if the roles are reversed, if a husband chooses to cheat on his wife.

> *When the question is about where the blame lies for committing adultery, the biblical focus is upon the spouse who sinned and not the partner who was sinned against.*

Throughout God's word, God consistently judges the **actions** of the actors (see 2 Corinthians 5:10). The reason the husband is not to blame is that *he did not commit adultery.*

Since this is a consistent message throughout the Bible—that we alone are responsible for our own actions and sins—that begs the question:

Why Does The Shared Responsibility Lie Persist?

I have a few theories for why this lie persists, even in the church:

1) The lie is built upon a twisted truth.

The most powerful lies are the ones Satan seeds with a little truth. That is how Satan baits the hook to entice people to swallow the deadly lie.

In this case, the lie about shared responsibility trades on the truth that relationships take two people, and we all bring sin into any relationship, as all are sinners (see Romans 3:23). That is the tantalizing bait. *It is all true.*

Where things get demonically twisted is extending these truths to mean that both parties must always contribute to the execution of a given sin in the marriage. *That is false.*

We are responsible for our own choices and actions—whether married or not.

It only takes one spouse to decide to commit adultery. And it only takes one spouse to decide to discard his or her marriage vows and abandon his or her family. The choices and actions are fully upon the soul of the one choosing such sin.

Another way things get demonically twisted is extending those truths to mean sins in a marriage cause adultery or infidelity, as if such sins absolve the cheater in part.

To be clear:

Circumstances—even sinful marital circumstances—do not cause sins. Sinners cause sin.

The **marriage**—i.e., the relationship—is *not* what answers to God on Judgment Day (see 2 Corinthians 5:10). Rather, the **individuals** in said marriage are the ones who have to give an accounting for their own actions.

Blaming your spouse or Satan for your own actions will not work on that Day.

2) Believing The Shared Responsibility Lie fosters an illusion of control and safety from vulnerability.

If you are partially responsible, then that means you have—or had—some control over protecting your marriage from its violation or implosion.

This is a false assurance.

Cheated On

The truth is each of us are vulnerable to the sin of our spouses. We can no more control their actions than we can control the inner workings of their hearts and minds.

This fact is scary, and to avoid facing such vulnerability, Christians believe and promulgate The Shared Responsibility Lie. People often are willing to settle for false security rather than face the harsh realities of their real vulnerability in this sin-torn world. From a pastoral perspective, this piles on additional, unwarranted shame for the faithful spouse who is vulnerable and potentially contributes to a dangerous false hope that he or she can control another person into being faithful.

3) Believing and promoting The Shared Responsibility Lie strokes some people's pride.

> "See how smart I am?! I can see both sides of this issue, and like the marriage 'experts' say: 'It takes two to tango.'"
> – Smartypants Christian

As a pastor myself, I can see this line of thinking being especially alluring for ministers who feel intellectually insecure. They seek the validation of playing psychologist in this area, selling their biblical birthright of godly wisdom for a porridge of putrid soup, but this is all about ego and image.

Supporting The Shared Responsibility Lie is simply the easy option for pastors. Truly courageous and biblical pastoral care providers swim against the stream of pop-psychology where blame for sins is distributed between *both* the victim and the perpetrator of adultery.

Besides pastors or elders, other Christians might support the lie for another prideful reason. They may do this because it makes them look morally superior to the faithful spouse. They may suffer from petty insecurities and may need to put people down to make themselves feel better, even if that person has suffered grievous wounds.

These individuals utilize The Shared Responsibility Lie and say the faithful spouse experienced soul rape because of their own moral failings.

The implied message here is that *they* have not experienced soul rape because *they* are morally superior to the faithful spouse.

> They know how "to keep their man (or woman)," or so these Christians think.

Pride blinds such Christians.

They fail to see the truth that the faithful spouse may very well be morally superior to *them*, as soul rape can happen to anyone, including the righteous. *(Just ask the Old Testament prophet Hosea.)*

> "Be of sober spirit, be on the alert. Your adversary, the devil, prowls around like a roaring lion, seeking someone to devour."
> – 1 Peter 5:8, NASB

Many other dynamics keep this lie circulating within the Christian community, but these three theories offer at least some initial context.

One last thing worth noting:

Satan, the "Father of Lies," has a vested interest in keeping The Shared Responsibility Lie alive and active. I am certain that he is stoking the fires as well, for this lie causes untold pain and suffering to its victims and the community.

We should never forget:

We are in a spiritual war!
Satan certainly does not forget.

# Chapter 3
A Godly Divorce

A God-honoring divorce? *Does such a thing exist? Or are all divorces sinful, God-defying actions?*

I assure you that *some* divorces are *very* godly.

Verses from both the Old and New Testament testify to this theological truth:

Sometimes divorce is a reasonable and righteous response to sin.

> I will argue in this chapter that godly Christians ought to default to divorce—under certain circumstances—if they are truly committed to following God faithfully.

Before exploring arguments from Scripture on behalf of *some* divorces, I want to point out the pitfalls of the position that claims that divorce is never acceptable among Christians.

I consider a position of an absolute divorce prohibition highly irresponsible, regardless of who promotes it.

Yet this divorce prohibition stance is a common one among Christians. Most people are familiar with it, and they may assume—falsely—that anything less is unchristian.

However, the "never divorce" position comes with nasty baggage:

> When divorce is always unacceptable, everything else is consequently acceptable in a marriage—including ongoing adultery and all sorts of other destructive abuse!

Such a position encourages spouses to stay in life-threatening situations even though they may be in imminent danger. This creates a perverse situation in which divorce is somehow worse than anything else, even life-threatening abuse.

By promoting a "never divorce" stance as the only biblical stance, the faithful spouse's faith community uses the threat of God's disapproval of divorce to keep them from taking actions of self-preservation. The threat of formal or even informal community censure keeps many faithful spouses stuck in destructive marriages.

> Something is truly amiss with a "Christian" position when it promotes life-threatening, sin tolerance rather than sin confrontation and godly consequences.

As the author of Ecclesiastes writes (see 3:1), in this sin-torn world, everything has a season...*even divorce.*

Sometimes the wisest and most righteous choice is to divorce an adulterous spouse.

God's own actions toward his unfaithful people, Israel, make this clear. Besides this powerful metaphorical example in the Old Testament, the details of one man's choice to divorce in the New Testament furthers supports this stance toward adultery.

First, consider God's example in the book of Jeremiah, in which God is presented as the faithful husband dealing with a remorseless adulteress, Israel.

How does God respond to this situation?

> "I gave faithless Israel her certificate of divorce and sent her away because of all her adulteries."
> – Jeremiah 3:8a, NIV

God divorces adulterous Israel. That is what the text tells us. It is right there for anyone to see. Some Christians may try to argue that this is not a "real" divorce, since God takes back Israel in the end.

Cheated On

This argument fails for three reason:

First, the verse plainly states that God issues a divorce certificate to Israel. Those arguing against this being a divorce must convince others the word "divorce" does not mean "divorce" in this verse. Any success in doing so leaves all of Scripture open to such reinterpretation where the reader gets to redefine words based on their ideology and *not* on what those words actually mean.

Second, God taking Israel back is more analogous to a remarriage than to never divorcing Israel in the first place. Sometimes people remarry spouses whom they previously divorced.

A remarriage to the same spouse does not mean the divorce never happened.

God taking Israel back does not mean God never divorced Israel. Both can be true. God divorced Israel and then took them back.

Third, those arguing against this as a real divorce by God are not consistent as it comes to the eternal destiny of Israel. If God never really divorced Israel, then that means all of Israel—past, present, and future—will be in Heaven as God's Bride. Those denying this is a real divorce generally do not take this position.

They do not take this position for good reason: Scripture does not support it. The Apostle Paul clearly states the salvation of all of Israel is *not* the case in his teaching in Romans 11. Some of Israel was broken off permanently from God (see Romans 11:19-21).

A real divorce has occurred for those in Israel who have rejected God. By their unbelief, God has decided to break them off from the blessings of the covenant.

So, one must either agree with the Apostle Paul in Romans 11 or deny the divorce ever occurred in Jeremiah 3:8a. You cannot hold both positions and remain consistent.

With this nonsense that "divorce" does not mean "divorce" in Jeremiah 3:8 addressed, the major theological implications of a verse in which God actively engages in divorce can be fully explored.

God is described as engaging in a divorce.
This explodes the idea of divorce as always sin!

> Because God divorces Israel per Jeremiah 3:8, this means divorce under some situations is de facto godly, in the sense that one is behaving like God by divorcing a spouse.

A perfect God cannot sin, even metaphorically. Therefore, divorce under some circumstances must *not* be sin.

What were the metaphorical circumstances in Jeremiah 3?

The circumstances of this divorce in Jeremiah 3:8 are that a spouse is remorselessly engaging in adultery. God decides that this abusive, idolatrous behavior will not be tolerated. Consequently, God, who is always holy and righteous, divorces Israel.

Plenty of faithful spouses have partners who exhibit the same remorselessness as Israel did in Jeremiah's day. They are faced with a choice of continuing to tolerate the ongoing infidelity and abuse or of using divorce to release their adulterous partner to go down his or her spiritually destructive path alone.

> I suggest divorce is a better option than tolerance of ongoing infidelity and abuse.
> It's an option even God exercised.

The example of God in Jeremiah 3:8 suggests that divorcing adulterous spouses is a godly action. God was not ashamed to take such action. A faithful spouse need not be ashamed of divorcing a cheating partner, either.

Cheated On

The act of refusing to enable or tolerate marriage-defiling and God-defying behavior is not shameful. It is a stance that affirms God's insistence on righteousness and fidelity in marriage.

But the Old Testament is hardly the only place in which such a godly approach to divorce is demonstrated. This posture also takes place in the New Testament. In fact, a famous passage in the Gospel of Matthew has *major* implications for a godly theology of divorce.

> "Because Joseph her husband was faithful to the law, and yet did not want to expose her to public disgrace, he had in mind to divorce her quietly."
> – Matthew 1:19, NIV

The verse in Matthew comes from the story about Jesus' birth in which Joseph responds to the news about Mary's miraculous pregnancy by the Holy Spirit.

For those tempted to write off this verse as applicable only for engagement periods, I want to remind you:

Engagements do not end with divorce.
Only marriages end with divorce.

"Divorce" is the correct translation for the word used here. ***Joseph had resolved to <u>divorce</u> a pregnant Mary.***

Clearly, the relationship between Mary and Joseph was considered just as binding back then as a modern marriage is today, since it required a divorce for it to end.

How does the Bible describe a man who has discovered—under natural circumstances—his partner has been sexually unfaithful?

Does Matthew describe Joseph as "sinful" or "wicked" in resolving to divorce Mary? ***No.***

Does Matthew describe Joseph as "hard-hearted" in resolving to divorce Mary? ***No.***

Rev. David Derksen

Does Matthew describe Joseph as "morally weak" in resolving to divorce Mary? No.

On the contrary, the actual Greek word used to describe Joseph is more properly translated "righteous" as opposed to "faithful to the law," as the NIV renders that word.

Righteous.

Resolving to divorce an (apparently) adulterous partner is considered the behavior of a righteous spouse. Let that thought sink into your psyche.

The faithful spouse is not described in negative terms whatsoever for making this choice! Joseph is forever memorialized in Scripture as a righteous man for choosing divorce under these circumstances.

> This is why I argue defaulting to divorce under adulterous circumstances is characteristic of a person who is righteous and God-honoring.

The book of Hosea was already written by the time these events transpired (more on the book of Hosea later), so the image of a forgiving husband welcoming back an adulterous wife would have been familiar within Jewish culture.

Yet Matthew does not use the example of Hosea to portray Joseph's response to Mary's pregnancy in a negative moral light.

He does not use this resolution to divorce Mary as an occasion to shame a faithful spouse and make an example of such "ungodly" behavior.

Rather, Matthew uses very positive language to describe Joseph *for resolving to divorce a pregnant Mary!*

> Choosing divorce appears to be the assumed righteous response to a sexually unfaithful partner here in the New Testament.

I submit that the modern Church has lost this biblical understanding.

Instead of starting at a place of assuming divorce in matters of adultery, we assume marriage reconciliation and restoration.

Cheated On

We shame faithful spouses for choosing to divorce remorseless cheaters, rather than following the Gospel example here of praising them for taking a righteous stance against adultery.

Christians need to return to assigning positive character traits to someone who desires to honor and enforce consequences regarding God's most basic moral laws.

We need to follow Matthew's example by applauding faithful spouses as righteous when choosing not to tolerate adultery.

> Divorce ought to be the default position assumed of righteous spouses confronting adultery.

Two important things happen when we make this shift:

First, it strongly affirms the important and biblical message that adultery is *that* serious.

The Christian community should see such sin alone as warranting the ending of a marriage. Instead of expecting Christians to pressure and shame faithful partners for choosing to divorce cheaters, this shift in stance sends a different message:

The shift puts cheaters on notice that the Christian community will support the faithful spouse who chooses to righteously divorce over the cheater's unrighteous infidelity.

Adultery will not be tolerated or enabled in such a community. All will see a healthier and more godly view of divorce modeled when divorce is treated as less problematic than committing adultery.

Second, this divorce stance shift helps the Christian community regain a godly understanding of mercy.

The never-divorce crowd creates an environment that facilitates cheater entitlement. A cheater need not repent if he or she is "entitled" to stay married to the faithful spouse per the never-divorce teaching.

This is *highly* unhealthy and ungodly. It does not foster healthy relationships or godly marriages.

> *When divorce is assumed as the godly response to adultery, a cheater—and the Christian community—is taught that remaining in such marriages is an act of mercy from the faithful spouse.*

A cheater loses all claims to the benefits of their marriage when they choose to defile the marriage covenant by committing adultery (see Hebrews 13:4). A faithful spouse acts in mercy by choosing to stay in the marriage and not take away the benefits of marriage, even though they have the right to do so.

This puts the actors in the proper positions regarding sin and the need for repentance, as well as the rebuilding of trust:

> *No longer is the onus upon the faithful spouse to "win back" the cheater, but rather the onus is upon the cheater to repent out of gratitude for the faithful spouse's mercy in not divorcing him or her.*

I can almost hear the objections to this assumption:

Christians wailing about how "God *hates* divorce."

This leads to the next section of this book:

Troublesome Texts.

One of the most misunderstood verses in all of Scripture, Malachi 2:16, is where we will begin.

Chapter 4
Malachi 2:16—But God Hates Divorce!

> "'For I hate divorce,' says the LORD, the God of Israel, 'and him who covers his garment with wrong,' says the LORD of hosts. 'So take heed to your spirit, that you do not deal treacherously.'"
> – Malachi 2:16, NASB

Whenever Christians talk about divorce, this is generally the first verse that comes to mind. Sadly, this verse is just as misunderstood and misapplied as Jesus' teaching not to judge others.

Let me explain:

In properly drawing applicable lessons from any verse, the context of the verse matters greatly. This is especially true of this particular verse.

When this verse is isolated from its immediate literary context as well as the cultural context of its day, the natural consequence is the theological distortion that God rejects all divorce as odious behavior. This is a false conclusion.

When read in the context of its surrounding verses, a picture appears that is very consistent with God as portrayed in Jeremiah 3:8. The statement in Malachi 2:16 demonstrates that God takes adultery very seriously—perhaps more seriously than divorce.

This is the context of Malachi 2:16:

God is calling Jewish men to account for abusing the mercy of divorce to legitimize what amounts to adultery in the eyes of God.

This is not a polemic against divorce per se. It has a very specific target:

Malachi is targeting Jewish men who discarded their Jewish wives via divorce to marry (likely younger) pagan wives.

Malachi is addressing the wickedly inventive ways of humans who obey the letter of the law while violating the spirit. Divorce is clearly sinful if done simply to obtain a more desirous spouse—e.g., a younger, pagan spouse in this case.

The Jewish men of Malachi's time abused the mercy of divorce in order to maintain a veneer of righteousness while acting on the adultery in their hearts.

God hates adultery so much that He is willing to condemn the vehicle (i.e., divorce) being used to facilitate this evil.

Context matters. When context is forgotten or ignored, Christians misuse this verse and thereby spiritually abuse faithful spouses who seek divorce from adulterous ones.

Using this verse to condemn all divorce ignores the historical and theological context of Malachi's day. *God's people were still under the Law as given by Moses.*

Malachi 2:16 is not about faithful spouses seeking an end to their marriages to cheaters—such a divorce in Malachi's day would have been completely unnecessary per the Old Testament law's teaching to kill the adulterous parties! (Deuteronomy 22:22)

Another reason why applying Malachi 2:16 as a blanket prohibition against divorce is unbiblical is the way it mistakenly describes God's priorities. It says,

"Divorce is more shameful than lying and committing adultery."

This is blatantly false. Lying and committing adultery both make the list of prohibited sins in the Ten Commandments (e.g., Exodus 20). *Yet choosing divorce does not.*

Divorce is not always sin, as we discussed in chapter three, for God is described as divorcing Israel (Jeremiah 3:8) and God does not sin.

Any interpretation and application of Malachi 2:16 that treats a potentially non-sin, divorce, as worse than an always-sin, adultery, is a poor interpretation and application.

A better and more biblically consistent interpretation of Malachi 2:16 teaches that God rejects the abuse of His mercy (the allowance of divorce in some circumstances) to pursue sin—namely, the sin of adultery.

One final analogy:

God hates divorce like some people hate prisons. Prisons are broken, miserable places that are easily abused. But they are necessary precisely because allowing people to freely commit crimes is far, far worse.

Divorce is awful. It is not God's design. God certainly hates broken human relationships. But the hatred of divorce is akin to a hatred of prison. The problem is the "crime"—e.g., adultery—*not* the "prison."

But what about the case of Hosea taking back the adulterous Gomer? Does that not prove that God expects His followers to always take back an adulterous spouse regardless of that spouse's state of repentance?

This case is presented in the book of Hosea. And that is the next TROUBLESOME TEXT I will tackle.

Rev. David Derksen

Chapter 5
Book of Hosea—Marriage Advice, Really?

"When the LORD began to speak through Hosea, the LORD said to him, 'Go, marry a promiscuous woman and have children with her, for like an adulterous wife this land is guilty of unfaithfulness to the LORD.'"
– Hosea 1:2, NIV

"Then the LORD said to me, 'Go again, love a woman who is loved by her husband, yet an adulteress, even as the LORD loves the sons of Israel, though they turn to other gods and love raisin cakes.' So I bought her for myself for fifteen shekels of silver and a homer and a half of barley. Then I said to her, 'You shall stay with me for many days. You shall not play the harlot, nor shall you have a man; so I will also be toward you.'"
– Hosea 3:1-3, NASB

A common Scripture reading and application error is to take a narrative and treat it as prescribing a moral command. For example, one might read about the Prophet Isaiah going around naked for three years and treat it as how followers of God ought to behave (see Isaiah 20). Thankfully, most have not fallen into this awful application error.

Absurd? Yes. However, we do it all the time with other less-obvious passages.

We need to be careful about reading commands into narrative or poetic works.

In my pastoral opinion, this error is committed when Christian leaders read the story of Hosea and Gomer as an example of how faithful spouses ought to respond to adultery.

This story is about an extreme situation. Adding the merciless burden of requiring faithful spouses to pursue their abusers while they are already struggling under the trauma of adultery discovery is unjustified.

Using Hosea to prohibit divorce for faithful spouses is spiritually abusive.

That interpretation is an abuse of the book to further a merciless agenda against divorce of any kind. It is a misuse of God's name to manipulate vulnerable faithful spouses by telling them falsely that they *must* endure ongoing adulterous abuse like Hosea did.

This is not God's heart on these matters!

In the rush to pressure faithful spouses into *not* divorcing their adulterous spouses, pastors—and well-meaning, yet wrong, Christians—ignore many important pieces from this book:

1. They ignore the fact that Hosea is called by God to marry a prostitute.

Hosea was not surprised Gomer acted the way she did. Being married to an unfaithful spouse is what Hosea signed up for by marrying Gomer.

Most faithful spouses enter into the opposite of such an arrangement, one in which we expect our spouse to keep their solemn marital vows of fidelity for the entirety of the relationship. The discovery of infidelity is a catastrophic surprise. Most would never marry a person knowing infidelity was inevitable.

The circumstances of most marriages are *far* from analogous to this famous marriage in Scripture, and this fact alone ought to be enough to warn a wise student of the Bible *not* to use this passage to prescribe advice to faithful spouses.

Cheated On

2. This was a special call from God to Hosea.

God does not command anyone else to knowingly marry someone engaged in such behavior. In fact, God warns us to do the opposite. He tells us not to be yoked together with someone who lives in lies and sin (see 2 Corinthians 6:14).

In fact, God warns us to *not even eat* with someone who calls himself or herself a Christian and lives in such a sexually immoral way (see 1 Corinthians 5:11). It is hard to marry or stay married to someone if you are not allowed to eat with them.

3. The book works only when understood as an extreme example.

This book is supposed to be shocking in the context of how adultery is *usually* treated (e.g., Deuteronomy 22:22). If Gomer (and an adulterous spouse by analogy) was entitled to marital reconciliation, God would not have told Hosea to buy Gomer back (Hosea 3:1). Hosea would just have done so as a faithful God-follower.

Furthermore, we would not be shocked to read how Hosea kept taking her back like God takes back his adulterous people. *We would expect it.*

To demand this behavior from God or a faithful spouse is arrogant entitlement.

We do not deserve God's mercy when he doesn't divorce us to Hell for our sins. And, tragically, some people will end up in that condition according to Scripture (more on that and reconciliation later).

Similarly, an adulterous spouse does not deserve and is not entitled to marital reconciliation. It is pure unmerited mercy and grace coming from the faithful spouse if they choose to stay in the marriage. God does not command it.

4. Those using this book as marriage advice ignore Hosea's instructions to Gomer not to continue in adulterous sin after he buys her back (see Hosea 3:3).

Even in this most extreme example of forgiveness and reconciliation, Hosea requires fidelity from Gomer. This is a healthy, important, and godly boundary to maintain in marriage. God does not want His people to be doormats who tolerate sin. *The infidelity must stop!*

5. Those using this book as marriage advice ignore the passages in this book that describe God punishing Israel for her adulteries.

In fact, I suggest a stronger case can be made from this book for punishing adultery than for ignoring the sin by "reconciling" without consequences.

Here are a few examples of God punishing Israel's adulteries:

> "The people love to offer sacrifices to me, feasting on the meat, but I do not accept their sacrifices. I will hold my people accountable for their sins, and I will punish them. They will return to Egypt. Israel has forgotten its Maker and built great palaces, and Judah has fortified its cities. Therefore, I will send down fire on their cities and will burn up their fortresses."
> – Hosea 8:13-14, NLT

> "You are destroyed, Israel, because you are against me, against your helper."
> – Hosea 13:9, NIV

6. Those using this book as marriage advice confuse forgiveness for reconciliation and thereby collapse the distinction between the two.

Cheated On

God forgives us our sins, as this book powerfully teaches. I believe that is a true and applicable lesson for us all. We need to forgive others as God forgives us.

However, reconciliation does not follow from our obligation to forgive as Christians (more on these concepts later). While we are to forgive those who wrong us, we do not have to reconcile with everyone.

Reconciliation takes two. Not everyone will be reconciled to God, yet God has provided forgiveness for all through His Son. Some will never accept this forgiveness.

It is not a deficiency in the faithful party that reconciliation has not taken place. God is not deficient because some choose a life of sin over a life of righteousness.

By choosing adultery, the adulterous spouse has chosen rebellion and relational death over fidelity and relational life.

7. An interpretation that requires taking back an adulterous spouse regardless of repentance fails to recognize our calling to be a holy people who do not tolerate sin.

Tolerance excuses and overlooks sin. It is not forgiveness; rather, tolerance traffics in a false spiritual reality where sin is "no big deal." In fact, holiness demands that the contamination of sin be addressed.

> "Like obedient children, do not be conformed to the desires that you formerly had in ignorance. Instead, as he who called you is holy, be holy yourselves in all your conduct; for it is written, 'You shall be holy, for I am holy.'"
> – 1 Peter 1:14-16, NRSV

The book of Hosea was never intended to provide marital advice for faithful spouses. It was not written to provide commands to pressure faithful spouses into reconciliation with their cheating spouses. That is an abuse of the book and an abuse of spiritual authority.

Rev. David Derksen

With two troublesome texts from the Old Testament addressed, we will now turn our attention to the New Testament. In particular, we will examine how a passage written as marriage advice from the Apostle Paul to the Ephesians is mishandled as well.

Chapter 6
Ephesians 5:21-33—Blame-Shifting at its "Finest"

> "Wives, submit yourselves to your own husbands as you do to the Lord.... Husbands, love your wives, just as Christ loved the church and gave himself up for her...."
> – Ephesians 5:22,25, NIV

I'm going to be transparent here:

This passage from Ephesians 5 bothers me. It does not bother me that it is in the Bible. I thank God for His Word. It is always true and trustworthy.

Rather, what bothers me about this passage is how I experienced it being used and how it continues to be used to abuse others in similar circumstances.

God's Word is life; the human interpretation and application of it is too often *not so much*.

Fortunately, I have heard sermons preached from evangelical pulpits that condemn the mishandling of this passage.

If a husband misunderstands and abuses this passage to dominate his wife, he is not loving her as Christ did the church. That is pretty obvious but has often been overlooked. I applaud my brother and sister ministers who expose the use of the submission teaching as an excuse to dominate and abuse.

While some evangelical pastors, thankfully, are starting to grasp how giving cover for domineering men is unhealthy and ungodly, they have not

Rev. David Derksen

all taken the next step to stomp out the blame-shifting in cases of infidelity.

This sort of subtle attack asserts or implies that the faithful wife was cheated upon *because* she was not properly submissive to her husband.

Such an attack is just as worthy of condemnation as the misuse of this passage to justify domineering husbands. *Both are abusive.*

The abuse of the Ephesians passage directed at faithful husbands comes with a different sort of twist.

I was alerted to this twist as I was preparing to defend my ministerial credentials with my former denomination. Let me explain this situation:

My former denomination was traditionally opposed to granting ministerial credentials to a pastor who is or was divorced. In fact, their 1982 policy explicitly prohibited it. They would strip the pastor—that is, defrock him—if that pastor divorced, no matter the circumstances.

Subsequently, they changed this policy and were willing to grant an "exception" if the pastor could demonstrate his divorce was "biblical"— for example, followed after the adultery of his wife. To obtain this "exception," the pastor had to go through a trial where evidence and various statements were submitted to a board determining ministerial standing.

This ecclesiastical trial requirement was in place when I successfully went through it. (In the end, they granted me an "exception" because the board of denominational officials were convinced from the submitted evidence that my ex-wife had committed adultery against me.)

When I was putting together my extensive evidence and statement for my ecclesiastical trial, my clinical pastoral education supervisor pointed out a possible assumption behind the proceedings apparent in the official denominational application guidelines.

She identified how the paperwork always put the male pastor (essentially only men are ordained in my former denomination) as responsible for what happened in the marriage. Therefore, the pastor was always responsible for the divorce *regardless of the circumstances.*

I see this as the unexamined fruit of an overly zealous application of "the husband is the head of the wife" teaching found in Ephesians 5:23ff (NIV).

An overzealous application of the truths in Ephesians regarding husband leadership leads to the conclusion:

The divorce is always the responsibility of the man—regardless of circumstances—because he is the head of the house.

This is a wicked teaching.

We are not responsible for another's sin (see Deuteronomy 24:16)! This truth is applicable to husbands as well as to wives.

> "Parents must not be put to death for the sins of their children, nor children for the sins of their parents. Those deserving to die must be put to death for their own crimes."
> – Deuteronomy 24:16, NLT

It is basic justice not to blame or hold accountable one person for the decisions or actions of another. *And God is just.*

Furthermore, God did not wring His hands wondering how he failed as a leader and "husband" while Israel played the harlot in the Old Testament (see Hosea 2). *He exhibits righteous anger.*

Then God divorces Israel when it is clear she will not stop her adulterous ways (Jeremiah 3:8). **God takes no blame for that divorce.**

Another problem with this nefarious and subtle teaching is how it undermines the wife's agency.

It obscures the reality that the Christian wife is accountable for her own actions and decisions. Realizing and taking responsibility for these decisions or actions are the prerequisites to repentance as one has to realize one's own power to choose differently in the future (i.e., to stop sinning).

> "For we must all appear before the judgment seat of Christ, so that each of us may receive what is due us for the things done while in the body, whether good or bad."
> – 2 Corinthians 5:10, NIV

This Scripture is important to keep in mind. The wife is still accountable for her actions. If she has committed adultery or abandoned her marriage without Biblical reasons, she has to answer to God for those sins. Those are actions. And "all" will appear before God for a reckoning.

I do not see God accepting the excuse on Judgment Day if a wife tries to blame her adultery on her husband by saying he was miserable at making her feel loved or was otherwise a "poor household leader."

God only has to point out that He is judging *her* actions, *not his*. Her husband did not commit adultery. She did. Now she must answer to God for *her own* actions.

Similarly, I do not see God accepting the excuse on Judgment Day if a husband tries to blame his adultery on his wife for her "lack of submission" to him.

God only has to point out that He is judging the husband's actions, *not hers*. His wife did not commit adultery. He did. Now he must answer to God for *his own* actions.

Spiritually, we will be ill-prepared for the Judgment Day if we teach or believe that spouses are not responsible for such serious actions as unbiblically divorcing or cheating on their partners. The wise Christian avoids any interpretation or application of Ephesians 5:22ff that teaches otherwise!

Cheated On

With the three most troublesome texts for faithful spouses addressed, we will turn our attention to several confounding concepts in the next section of the book. The first is framing recovery from infidelity as a matter primarily of healing through grief.

Chapter 7
Grief as Primary

> "My tears have been my food day and night, while people say to me all day long, 'Where is your God?'"
> – Psalm 42:3, NIV

Before exploring the confounding concepts of forgiveness or marriage reconciliation, we need to talk about grief.

In fact, I contend—even as an evangelical pastor—that attending to grief is the primary task for adultery victims, *not* attending to forgiveness of the cheater.

Remember: Adultery is soul rape.

This is a major, *major* trauma. Soul-level violence has been done to the faithful spouse, leaving deep, *deep* wounds.

As a general commonsense rule:

Deep wounds do not heal overnight.

Just as it is unhelpful and somewhat mean for a Christian to tell a stabbing victim to forgive his assailant while the victim is still gushing blood from the six-inch deep wound, it is both unhelpful and lacking compassion to tell an adultery victim to forgive the cheater without first attending to the deep grief wounds the cheater inflicted.

Oddly, Christians are quick to dismiss grief tasks in favor of focusing on "forgiveness" as if grief is unnecessary and somehow selfish. Unlike the writers of Scripture, modern Christians do not do lament well.

And trust me. The losses that come with discovering an unfaithful spouse are catastrophic. A cheater selfishly blows up the entire life of the faithful spouse by committing adultery.

The losses hit financial health, physical health, mental health, social health, and spiritual health, to name just a few categories assaulted at this time.

The Golden Rule of treating others as we would like to be treated is critical at this time. Insisting that another person jump straight to forgiveness before making an inventory of his or her losses strikes me as especially premature and cruel.

I would not recommend pressuring a rape victim to forgive her rapist immediately in the aftermath of said rape. Yet this happens all the time to soul rape victims. In fact, the assaults to their souls may not yet be at an end.

Now, I understand that this error—i.e., jumping ahead to instruct a faithful spouse to forgive—often comes from genuinely caring people.

So, the question is:

Why is skipping over the faithful spouse's grief so common among Christians?

Grief is uncomfortable. It is hard to sit with someone you love in their time of grief. Their pain becomes your pain. All you want to do is make the pain go away, yet you are truly powerless to do so.
Just as the faithful spouse was powerless to stop their partner from cheating on them, you are powerless to take away the losses—i.e., consequences—of such sin. *Powerlessness is a truly icky feeling.*

So, how do we help someone in the depths of infidelity-inflicted grief?

Many resources exist for those going through the process of grief. This book is not intended to replace those resources or to engage in a debate over Kübler-Ross's famous five stages of grief (denial, anger, bargaining, depression, and acceptance).[1]

As a reminder, this is a guidebook for fellow pastors and for those who can identify with the statement, "I was cheated on."

To such ends, I want to focus on a couple of key ideas related to the topic of grief that have the potential to truly help faithful spouses in these situations.

1) Remember that grief is a healthy response to loss.

All the crazy emotions of sadness, anger, and even happiness cycling through the aggrieved ought to be expected.

Normally, we would not expect less from a widowed spouse who just lost their partner due to some violent ending like a car crash. Make the same allowances for a faithful partner as their marriage—as they knew it—has met a violent end due to infidelity.

2) Remember that grief is an emotional—as opposed to cognitive—process.

We do not think our way out of grief. Rather, we must feel our way through these difficult emotions.

This is important to remember, both for the faithful spouse and for the outsider. Our emotions do not simply go away by willing them away. Patience is key here, as well as acknowledging the reality of these feelings.

Like a persistent child who needs to be heard, the emotions will not go away if simply ignored. *They must be heard and acknowledged.*

That said, you do not have to do what the inner child tells you to do. Letting your child know you see him or her is enough.

---

[1] Kübler-Ross, Elizabeth. (2011). *On Death and Dying: What the Dying Have to Teach Doctors, Nurses, Clergy & Their Own Families.* New York: Scribner. (Original work published 1969).

Cheated On

This is *not* a license to allow your anger, for example, to lead you into sin.

Rather, notice the "anger child" and acknowledge this "child's" existence in your heart. This sort of noticing work is part of the healing path of grief.

A related point is to remember we all grieve in our own ways, just as we all have unique ways our hearts respond to life's events. The important thing here is to suspend judgment when it comes to the emotions you are having as you go through the grief journey.

Third, remember that those grieving have experienced extreme injustice and as such ought to have anger over those violations.

Anger is not always bad. Yet we are called to keep from sinning out of our anger (see Ephesians 4:26).

The anger is a healthy source of energy for the faithful spouse. Properly channeled, the faithful spouse can use this energy to reset necessary personal boundaries.

A strong temptation exists for faithful spouses to deny the infidelity took place and suppress the anger that comes with acknowledging this truth. A true and godly friend will not participate in encouraging such a denial of reality. He or she will provide a safe space for the faithful spouse to acknowledge the reality and feel the anger. Faithful spouses need this space if they are to heal from the trauma. They need people who will not judge them for their righteous anger.

I think this is a place where outsiders fear the faithful spouse will get stuck. They worry the faithful spouse will trap themselves in loops of retelling the same betrayal story over and over again. So, they employ the "forgive them" strategy to disrupt this "loop."

I would like to remind you that such a tactic demonstrates its user has failed to truly grasp how grief is at play here. Telling the faithful spouse who is still processing the reality of what happened "to forgive" is a way to encourage emotional stuffing and denial.

45

It is not helpful.

The faithful spouse needs validation here. The fear of them becoming stuck is precisely the sort of barrier that will make it a self-fulfilling prophecy as they become stuck in a cycle of seeking validation that never comes.

They need someone who helps them face and grasp the ugly reality of the infidelity. The last thing a faithful spouse needs is someone denying this reality or telling them to ignore it.

> You cannot heal from catastrophic losses and injustices by ignoring them or denying they have taken place.

The injustices experienced by the faithful spouse do not disappear—along with all the feelings that go with them—simply by denying their occurrence or telling faithful spouses to ignore them. The journey to wholeness begins with seeing and naming the losses. Denial is not a life-giving, long-term strategy.

So, we acknowledge the injustice. The faithful spouse has had time to walk along the grieving journey. But what do we do with all these personal injustices faithful spouses experience? Is this where forgiveness enters the picture?

Possibly.

Christians are quick to say, "Forgive!" This is the next "Confounding Concept" I will tackle. Too often, we have a distorted or unhelpful grasp of what forgiveness is.

Cheated On

Chapter 8
Godly Forgiveness

> "For if you forgive others for their transgressions, your heavenly Father will also forgive you. But if you do not forgive others, then your Father will not forgive your transgressions."
> – Matthew 6:14-15, NASB
> "If your brother or sister sins against you, rebuke them; and if they repent, forgive them."
> – Luke 17:3b, NIV
> "Forgive as the Lord forgave you."
> – Colossians 3:13b, NIV

Christians—especially—have some serious misconceptions about what godly forgiveness is and is not. These misconceptions wreak havoc upon faithful spouses and contribute to much suffering.

Let's dig into a few of these misconceptions:

> **MISCONCEPTION #1:**
> **Forgiving means forgetting.**

When a rape victim forgives her rapist, does she forget what happened? *Should she?* I suggest it would be unwise for her to forget what took place. She *ought to* remember that this person is unsafe.

A faithful spouse has been soul raped and similarly ought to remember their soul rapist is unsafe, even after forgiving him or her. It is unwise to forget such history. Plus, as with the rape victim, such a traumatic experience is *not* the sort of thing a human can just decide to forget.

Remembering the cheater is unsafe leads me to the second misconception regarding forgiveness:

MISCONCEPTION #2:
Forgiveness entails reconciling.

Forgiveness is not reconciliation. It does not immediately restore trust and rebuild the relationship between the perpetrator and the forgiving victim.

The rape victim may truly forgive the rapist, yet that does not mean they should get back together as boyfriend and girlfriend.

Forgiveness does not restore the relationship to what it was before the perpetrator violated his victim. The same thing goes for soul rape victims and the adulterous offenders.

I will share more about reconciliation and restoration in the next chapter.

MISCONCEPTION #3:
Forgiveness means canceling any consequences for the sin.

If a child breaks his mother's priceless vase while playing catch in the living room, his mother will likely forgive him for doing so out of love for her child. However, the vase remains shattered. *Forever.*

The same idea goes for situations with infidelity.

One of the natural consequences of infidelity is the knowledge that one is married to someone who violated the most solemn of human vows—namely the marriage vows of fidelity. Forgiveness does not change or erase this truth. The "vase" remains shattered.

Forgiveness does not alter physical reality either. If the cheater picked up a sexually transmitted disease (STD) from an affair partner and passed it along to an unsuspecting faithful spouse, forgiveness does not make the STD go away.

MISCONCEPTION #4:
Forgiveness means treating the matter like it never happened.

Whether or not the couple decides to stay married after infidelity, it will always be true that infidelity took place in that relationship. *It is historical fact.*

Forgiveness cannot alter historical fact.

Pretending it never happened is living a lie. Insisting faithful spouses remain silent about the cheating is encouraging them to lie by omission.

Such pressure is like telling someone to pretend to be someone they are not. Using such pressure on faithful spouses is incompatible with walking in the truth and light as Christ-followers.

While this is not the only true matter regarding the couple, it is an important piece of their marital history. Forgiveness does not rewrite that history.

It will always be true that infidelity ravaged that relationship, independent of the cheater's forgiveness status.

MISCONCEPTION #5:
Forgiveness means protecting the reputation of the offender.

The cheater is responsible for rebuilding their own reputation. If they had wanted a good reputation, then they ought to have behaved accordingly. When they chose to cheat, they chose the path of a poor reputation.

Their actions—which were evil and awful—are what damaged their reputation. People learning of those actions are simply people learning the cheater's true character. *Forgiveness does not entail lying about someone's true character.*

"Even a child is known by his doings, whether his work be pure, and whether it be right."

> – Proverbs 20:11, KJV

Faithful spouses sharing the ugly truth about what happened are not necessarily punishing their cheaters. They are sharing historical facts.

Can sharing unflattering historical details be used to punish someone? Yes.

However, sometimes the sharing of those details is very appropriate and necessary to understand a situation properly.

For example, knowing someone was being cheated on sheds new light upon sudden weight loss and the so-called "crazy" behavior of that person during this period.

Such sharing is often necessary for faithful spouses to find the support they need to heal from this wicked trauma.

The freedom to share their marriage story is an important component of the grieving and healing process. To deny faithful spouses this freedom is to deny victims access to healing.

Forgiving a cheater does not entail giving up access to understanding and support that only comes with another person knowing the basic facts of what happened.

I have shared a great deal about what godly forgiveness is not. You might be wondering,

"What is godly forgiveness, then?"

> "For if you forgive others for their transgressions, your heavenly Father will also forgive you. But if you do not forgive others, then your Father will not forgive your transgressions."
> – Matthew 6:14-15, NASB

> "If your brother or sister sins against you, rebuke them; and ***if they repent***, forgive them."

> – Luke 17:3b, NIV (emphasis added)

When talking about forgiveness, most Christians are aware of the Matthew passage where Jesus commands his followers to forgive. However, many are *unaware* of the Luke passage quoted above and the conditional nature of the command to forgive.

This raises an early question about godly forgiveness:

Is forgiveness conditional or unilateral—meaning requiring only the one forgiving to accomplish?

I say, "Yes."

It is both. Hence, this is a paradox.

In some sense, we can forgive someone all on our own. However, in another sense, they are not forgiven until they respond in repentance as Jesus instructs us in Luke 17:3.

How is this so?

The answer to this is found in Colossians 3:13b (NIV):

> "Forgive as the Lord forgave you."

How does Jesus, our Lord, forgive us? *He is our ultimate model of forgiveness, after all.*

Now, I believe God died for and forgave all sins of the world through Jesus' death upon the cross (see John 3:16, 1 Peter 3:18, etc.). **However, I believe this forgiveness is *effective* only for those who receive it humbly as a gift.**

In other words, we must repent in order to receive God's forgiveness and salvation from the due punishment for our sins (see Acts 2:38).

So, the whole world is forgiven of their sins by the unilateral actions of Jesus on the cross—in a sense. However, in another sense, everyone is forgiven *only if* they repent of their sins to accept Jesus' gift of forgiveness paid for on the cross.

This is the paradox.

Forgiveness is unilaterally available yet only becomes real forgiveness for the sinner if he or she repents.

God's forgiveness, therefore, is conditioned on repentance from the sinner in order for that forgiveness to be received.

Applying this understanding to infidelity situations, I see the faithful spouse's spiritual responsibility as one where we work to release the debt of the sin to God. God then judges whether or not the cheater repents and is then truly forgiven.

In other words, we make the forgiveness "available" from our end. Then it becomes a matter between the cheater and God whether or not the cheater will repent and experience that forgiveness.

I say that we "work at this" because I consider forgiveness as a process much like grief.

The choice to forgive—i.e., to let go of the role of judge and executioner—can happen in a moment. However, the feelings take time to truly take root in the heart, especially for serious injustices like adultery.

We may have to make the choice to forgive and let go of the punisher role many, *many* times. I know I did. It usually takes some time for the feelings to catch up to our choices in such matters.

So, we need to do something regarding forgiveness to honor Christ's command, even if the cheater never repents and receives the forgiveness.

How do we put this into practice practically?

Practically, what helped me in the forgiveness process was actually making a list of the wrongs committed against me.

Making that list helped me in my grieving process as well. Having the wrongs written out helped the reality sink into my heart. Plus, you cannot forgive these things if you do not know what you are forgiving.

Another tip is to get your body involved in the process.

One way is to burn the list of wrongdoings. Delete the file. Every time I felt anger toward the offender, I would reach up in the air and make a hammering motion to remind myself that I had chosen to forgive and had placed those sins on Christ's cross.

Whatever you choose to do, be kind to yourself during this process.

Your feelings of anger toward the wrongdoer probably will not change overnight. Like me, you will likely have to do these things more than once. It may take years for the feelings of anger to subside.

But trust me, the anger does eventually subside. In its place, I have found a sense of pity toward those who wronged me. They must live with what they did to me and answer to God for that (see 2 Corinthians 5:10).

I do not envy their position.

> "For we must all stand before Christ to be judged. We will each receive whatever we deserve for the good or evil we have done in this earthly body."
> – 2 Corinthians 5:10, NLT

I draw two final lessons about forgiveness from a powerful little book in the Old Testament. The story about a prophet named Jonah follows his frustration with God's mercy toward the evil Ninevites.

Don't Build a Smiting Shelter!

> "Jonah had gone out and sat down at a place east of the city. There he made himself a shelter, sat in its shade and waited to see what would happen to the city."

Cheated On

> – Jonah 4:5, NIV

Jonah wanted to watch God punish the Ninevites for their wicked deeds. He made a "smiting shelter" so he would have front row seats to the show. And he was ready for God to execute justice to its fullest extent.

But God didn't.

He had mercy on the Ninevites. Jonah did not get the smiting show his heart so desired.

The Ninevites received God's mercy, because they humbled themselves and repented of their sin (see Jonah 3:6-10).

Forgiveness means we do not build "smiting shelters."

We hand over our grievances and hurts to God *fully*. Then we "walk" away.

We do <u>not</u> build proverbial places to observe God's hellfire raining down upon our cheating ex and company for what they have done to us (and our kids).

The example of Jonah reminds us that such building is improper behavior for God's people.

Yet this negative lesson is not the only lesson to learn from the story of Jonah and the Ninevites:

God is not very hard on Jonah for failing to extend mercy as quickly as God did.

God does not strike him dead on the spot for building a smiting shelter. He uses the situation to teach Jonah a lesson by sending a worm to destroy the shade-giving plant covering his smiting shelter (see the rest of chapter 4).

God is very patient with the ones He loves. He dearly loves us, faithful spouses. So, my point here is to cut yourself some slack if you spent time building your own smiting shelter.

God is patient.

He does not condemn the ones He has redeemed.

God lovingly and gently corrects His children.

Now, with a fuller understanding of godly forgiveness and how to practice it, we can explore what godly reconciliation or marriage restoration is.

Cheated On

Chapter 9
Righteous Restoration And Reconciliation

> "He [John the Baptist] went into all the country around the Jordan,
> preaching a baptism of repentance for the forgiveness of sins."
> – Luke 3:3, NIV

The Biblical order is repentance first and then forgiveness (see Luke 17:3). That was the order presented by John the Baptist, who led the way for Jesus' ministry. And that is the order we need to follow if we are to honor God with marriage reconciliation.

Repentance first, forgiveness second, and *then—only then—* marriage restoration third.

I believe this order is scrambled in Christian communities because so much emphasis is placed on *not* divorcing.

Avoiding the divorce outcome has become more important to some Christians than ensuring true repentance on the part of the cheater. This is out of line with how God relates to His covenant people.

> "Then Samuel said to all the people of Israel, 'If you want to return to the LORD with all your hearts, get rid of your foreign gods and your images of Ashtoreth. Turn your hearts to the LORD and obey him alone; then he will rescue you from the Philistines.'"
> – 1 Samuel 7:3, NLT

Here we see God talking about the need for repentance. God is willing to forgive and restore the relationship, *but God requires a true turning of Israel from her idols*. He requires an end to Israel's idolatrous adulteries. And He requires proof via action on the part of Israel.

A godly reconciliation—i.e., marriage restoration—after infidelity requires following this healthy boundary model. This is the *sine qua non—i.e., essential prerequisite—* of godly marriage restoration.

Complete turning from the adultery partner with action-based proof is necessary for even a chance at godly marriage restoration.

How might that look?

Here are a few suggestions:

- A complete and total owning of choices and sinful actions, without exception; this is a necessary first step.
- Complete openness, with willingness to answer any question from the faithful spouse (including more than once).
- Freely given permission for the faithful spouse to share about the infidelity with whomever they wish.
- No more being Facebook friends with the Other Man (OM) or Other Woman (OW).
- No keeping of the extramarital lover's gifts.
- No keeping of the extramarital lover's secrets from one's spouse.
- No more coffee dates or drinks after work with OM/OW.
- The cheater finds another job or moves location/department if the OM/OW is going to remain at the same workplace.

A change in actions is needed.

Evangelical pastors and elders, of all people, ought to stand firm in supporting this boundary for faithful spouses. I maintain that they ought to insist on it as part of providing sound biblical counsel for couples dealing with a marriage violated by infidelity.

After all, if God required action-based evidence of repentance from unfaithful Israel, why would we not follow God's own example in a similar situation?

Another important matter to keep in mind is that an over-commitment to marriage restoration is dangerous. Reconciliation or marriage restoration at all costs is dangerous.

It misses a harsh reality:

> Divorce is NOT the worst outcome following adultery!

The worst-case scenario is a cheater who refuses to repent, stays in a marriage continuing to abuse the faithful spouse, and spiritually experiences the hellfires of damnation for refusing to repent (see Hebrews 10:26-27).

That scenario can occur within the confines of a so-called "reconciled" marriage. *It is an outcome worth striving to avoid.*

The priority needs to be repentance first, then talk of forgiveness and restoration (of trust and *maybe* the marriage).

When pastors or other Christians push reconciliation with no reference to repentance, they are pushing an agenda out of line with the God's plan for restoring relationships. A sure sign of such ungodly priorities is talk of marriage reconciliation with the faithful spouse without reference to the cheater engaging in robust repentance as a precondition.

> *Reconciled and restored marriages are not on the table for faithful Christians as long as the cheater refuses to repent.*

The only godly restored marriages are the ones where real repentance is present on the part of the cheater.

Sometimes cheaters do exhibit or seem to exhibit robust, real repentance. *How do we handle or evaluate those situations in a godly fashion?*

Cheated On

Let's dig into a few practical ways to assess whether you have real or fool's gold when it comes to cheater repentance.

What are some signs of true repentance to keep you from being played for a fool again?

1. Humility.

Essentially, humility in this context is the cheater's willingness to accept full responsibility for cheating and their acknowledgment that staying in the marriage is an incredible, gracious gift given to them by the faithful partner. *A humble person puts others before himself or herself.*

The truly humble cheater is a person looking to care for the needs of the faithful spouse first. They are willing to bear the emotional and other costs to help the faithful spouse heal.

Let me provide a few examples of what humility does *not* look like:

- *If the cheater is spending couple's counseling going over the faithful spouse's "faults" (a.k.a., "what drove the cheater to cheat"), the cheater is not humble.*
- *If the cheater refuses to hear about the pain he or she caused the faithful partner and cites being "forgiven for all that already," the cheater is not humble.*
- *If the cheater demands to stay married and twists Scripture to manipulate the faithful partner, he or she is not humble.*
- *If the cheater spends the time with the marriage counselor or pastor mourning the loss of the affair partner or talking about how this so hard for them in the presence of their spouse, he or she is not humble.*

Also, a cheater freely and humbly submits to STD tests and shares the test results with his or her spouse as part of humbly accepting

Rev. David Derksen

what they did to the marriage and assuring the faithful spouse of his or her physical safety.

In my opinion, this is a very basic level of demonstrated care for the faithful spouse to help them feel less afraid of what life-threatening diseases the cheater may have exposed them to as a result of their cheating.

2. Restitution.

> "And Zacchaeus stood, and said unto the LORD: Behold, Lord, the half of my goods I give to the poor; and if I have taken any thing from any man by false accusation, I restore him fourfold."
> – Luke 19:8, KJV

To commit adultery is to lie and steal. The unfaithful partner has stolen time, money, and memories. They may have also tarnished or otherwise damaged the faithful spouse's reputation. These need to be restored to the best of the cheater's ability.

> *Like Zacchaeus in Luke 19, the cheater who is truly repentant for wronging the faithful spouse will go out of their way to make up for cheating their partner out of so much.*

In a secular legal system, we award damages that compel wrongdoers to pay back what they took and provide financially when what was stolen can never be returned (e.g., a damaged reputation). *This is what is considered just.*

To be a just and godly people, we ought to follow this principle regarding infidelity as well. *Justice demands restitution in these matters.*

Someone who has cheated but is now truly humble and repentant will have no objection to making restitution for their theft.

Restitution may take various forms in this matter:

- *The cheater ought to do their best to repair the damaged relationships with others their lies created in regard to the faithful partner.*
- *Money spent on the affair partner(s) ought to be repaid to the faithful partner.*
- *Trips taken together—i.e., stolen memories and finances—ought to be provided for the faithful partner as a way to make things right again (probably to a different location, though).*
- *Stolen intimacy—i.e., secrets with the affair partner—need to be exposed to the light for the faithful partner to see and know as well.*
- *The cheating partner needs to be willing to take their partner's justified anger and hurt over the cheating, stealing, and lying for as long as it takes for the faithful partner to heal from the cheater's treachery (and that timetable is determined by the faithful spouse alone).[2]*

Whether or not a cheater engages freely in acts of restitution is a way to see if the cheater is just saying "sorry" or is truly willing to put actions behind their "sorry."

To be clear:

A cheater unwilling or reluctant to engage in acts of restitution is an unrepentant cheater.

---

[2] Some might argue an experienced pastor or qualified counselor ought to set this timetable. I do not agree. That is like saying a pastor or counselor gets to set your grieving period, and if you need more time outside that period, you are in the wrong. It is a controlling and cognitive approach to an emotional process. The faithful spouse is uniquely positioned to know when he or she is ready to move on in the process from this stage. A pastor can provide feedback and counsel but ought never to have the power to set the timetable for the faithful spouse's healing. That is theirs alone to determine, along with the Holy Spirit.

3. Transparency.

> **Cheating is all about hiding treacherous deeds in the dark.**
> *Transparency is of utmost importance in light of this reality.*

The cheater no longer gets the benefit of the doubt. They abused that benefit to wicked ends and therefore ought to understand the need for the faithful partner to always know or have access to their whereabouts, phone, and online activities.

> *Transparency includes sharing what the cheater did as many times as the faithful spouse needs.*

Grief is not a one-and-done sort of thing. It takes considerable time to process deep wounds, and infidelity leaves deep wounds.

The faithful spouse needs to know both cognitively *and emotionally* what was lost, and part of that knowing requires reviewing the wrongs done to them. It might take time and repeated conversations before the awful reality is seen, accepted, and healed.

Using the faithful spouse's commitment to "forgiveness"—as in, *"These things were already forgiven and ergo no longer ought to be mentioned"*—short-circuits this important grieving process. It is akin to telling the faithful spouse that they ought not to feel a certain way. The deep injury of infidelity does not heal overnight, and even after it heals, the once broken "bone" still aches in certain seasons. Invoking forgiveness language to shut down faithful spouses and deny them the emotional space to heal and grieve is wrong. It is spiritual abuse.

When "forgiveness" is invoked to shut down sharing about the infidelity, this says the invoker's discomfort over discussing the infidelity takes priority over the faithful spouse's need to heal and grieve. *That is not humble.* A cheater engaging in such behavior is a cheater who is not repentant.

4. Freely and Actively Attending Counseling.

Cheating is caused by a character flaw in the cheater. The lies and entitlement must be mercilessly destroyed and uprooted in the cheater's heart (e.g., Hebrews 12:4).

A repentant cheater realizes this need and willingly gets *appropriate* help. They do not wait upon the faithful spouse's initiative in making an appointment but do so themselves as they realize their great need for such help.

A note of caution:

Not all counselors—or pastors for that matter—are equipped to deal with such scenarios. The last thing one needs is a pastor or counselor who enables blame-shifting and entitlement-mentality in the cheater.

> *A cheater does not need more sophisticated excuses for why they cheated, but rather someone who holds them fully responsible for choosing sin and encourages them to change their ways.*

Cheaters also do not need a pastor or counselor who is wrapped around the cheater's finger and a willing participant in the cheater's pity-party.

Instead, they need a pastor or counselor to treat such pity-parties as what they are:

A toddler tantrum over cleaning up a mess that the toddler made on their own.

A naïve pastor or counselor is no good either.

They need a healthy amount of skepticism directed toward whatever the cheater says, since the cheater is a proven liar. Words need to be verified with actions as the cheater has squandered the benefit of the doubt by being unfaithful.

Rev. David Derksen

The attitude the cheater has toward counseling is important to note as well.

A repentant cheater does not view this activity as externally imposed (e.g., "She's making me go to counseling."). Rather, a repentant cheater views going to counseling as an opportunity to fix the mess they made.

In other words, counseling is treated as a lifeline to the cheater, as opposed to a punishment. A truly repentant cheater does not need to be convinced that they need professional help to change. They understand their issues are really *that bad!*

A repentant cheater views counseling as a way to better himself or herself independent of marriage status. They go because they realize they still need to change their character even if the marriage ends in divorce.

This is another important point:

The cheater is *not* entitled to marriage restoration in exchange for attending individual counseling!

A faithful spouse may still choose divorce after the cheater goes through all that therapy. *And that is okay.* I see no statute of limitations or conditions on Jesus' permission to divorce over sexual infidelity (see Matthew 19:9). Adultery is *that* devastating, and a truly repentant cheater understands this.

5. Binding Exit Agreement.

Someone has said that "past behavior is the best predictor of future behavior." It is the axiom given in suicide prevention training that I have attended. This axiom also applies to marriages ravaged by adultery.

It does not mean everyone will cheat again. However, the reality is that such cheating is more likely to happen again than not. A wise person accepts that reality and plans to deal with this probable worst-case scenario.

Cheated On

> *It is not just to insist the faithful spouse put themselves in a situation of vulnerability where they set themselves up to be victimized again.*

A binding exit agreement can be designed to mitigate such risk to the faithful spouse by providing them a generous financial exit and child custody stipulations in the event the faithful spouse decides reconciliation is not working for them. Another important piece is to make sure this agreement is totally actionable for the faithful spouse with or without additional cheating evidence. The faithful spouse does not need to stay around Biblically even if no further cheating happens. *(I am not a lawyer, so I would recommend finding a qualified legal professional to help you craft this properly.)*

Furthermore, a binding exit agreement sends a clear message that cheating will not be tolerated!

The agreement is a clear statement of consequences in the event the cheater decides to go back to their old wicked ways or simply refuses to do the work to rebuild the marriage.

This agreement is a completely unnecessary document in the event the cheater truly reforms and restores what they destroyed. A refusal to engage in the creation of such a document or sign it afterward says that the cheater wants the door left open to cheat without consequences; thus, that means the cheater really isn't repentant.

A repentant cheater understands that with or without the document, the faithful spouse has the option to legally end the marriage without spiritual censure due to the cheater's infidelity (see Matthew 19:9).

It is risky and extremely generous for a faithful spouse to give a cheater another chance in remaining married to them.

In some cases where cheater repentance is evident, I am aware that God does work miracles and resurrects marriages ravaged by deceit and adultery. However, I encourage people going through the restoration and rebuilding process to go forward with their eyes open.

67

Rev. David Derksen

Get some sort of binding exit agreement!

Reconciliation Versus Restoration

An important distinction exists between reconciliation and restoration. They are not the same thing.

A reconciled relationship is one where the hostilities have ceased. The relationship is "warm" again between the parties.

That does not necessarily mean the two parties are married, though.

The two parties could be reconciled *while remaining divorced*. The marriage may never be restored.

> Marriage restoration and reconciliation are two distinct things.

The faithful spouse may fully forgive and be reconciled with the cheater, yet the faithful spouse might decide to remain divorced as a matter of wisdom—i.e., they think it unwise to open themselves up to the possibility of a repeat adulterous-abuse performance.

To avoid collapsing this important distinction between reconciliation and restoration, I prefer to talk about marriages formerly ravaged by infidelity yet healed as "restored marriages."

> *Dealing with the devastation of infidelity in a marriage is not just a remodel of the marriage but a complete rebuild.*

Adultery causes extreme and severe damage to a marriage. *It kills innocence and whatever marriage one once had.*

Too often, I hear stories about pastors and "Christian" counselors approaching marriages ravaged by adultery as if the infidelity is merely a symptom and not a marriage-ending sin as Scripture teaches (e.g., Deuteronomy 22:22, Jeremiah 3:8, Matthew 1: 19, etc.).

Cheated On

Scripture teaches us that God views the faithful oneness of marriage as the foundation of a marriage. That oneness is violated—sometimes repeatedly—when adultery has taken place. A marriage ravaged by infidelity has to be rebuilt from the bottom up.

In other words, adultery destroys the marriage's fundamental foundation. Therefore, a godly marriage restoration *requires* a re-laying of that foundation with the foreign, destructive elements excluded from it this time around.

> "And every one that heareth these sayings of mine, and doeth them not, shall be likened unto a foolish man, which built his house upon the sand: And the rain descended, and the floods came, and the winds blew, and beat upon that house; and it fell: and great was the fall of it."
> – Matthew 7:26-27, KJV

Think of a marriage ravaged by adultery like a house:

> *Adultery burned down the house known as the marriage. In some cases, the "arsonist" added gasoline, tossed the match, and clapped with their "friends" as they watched the family "home" go up in a blaze.*

Sure, some people stay together after their marriage has been violated by infidelity. However, without rebuilding from the foundation up to directly address the damage done by the infidelity and deceit, the marriage will inevitably suffer from the destruction that comes from building on a cracked foundation.

Character issues in the cheater need addressing for the house to avoid succumbing to future collapse or other destruction—like from another adultery forest fire.

This is no small task. It is not like doing a simple painting job. Fundamentally rotten "materials"—namely the cheater's character—need addressing.

A wise person rips out the rotten studs in the walls. They do not just drywall over them. The same goes with addressing the rotten aspects of the cheater's character. They need to be eradicated first before restoring the home.

Can a marriage come back from something like that?

Yes, but it takes a lot of work, just as it takes a lot of work to rebuild a burned-out house. Only a foolish builder denies and underestimates the cost of restoring a house destroyed by such a fire.

The house may still have the same "address" —e.g., Bob and Jane Johnson—but the marriage "house" is not the same after adultery. Marriage restoration after infidelity is like a total gut job. You have to take it down to the "studs" and possibly further.

> The marriage can never be the same after the fires of adultery and deception have had their way with the original "residence."

The cost is steep to undergo such an involved restoration process—and that assumes the basic material of a truly repentant cheater is at hand. Some cheaters will decide not to do the hard work of character transformation that makes such a restoration possible in the first place.

At the same time, remember:

According to Jesus Himself, it is perfectly acceptable for the faithful spouse to decline to engage in such a restoration process (see Matthew 5:32 and 19:9).

With reconciliation and restoration addressed, we next turn to the difficult topic of children caught in the mess of infidelity and possibly divorce. This is the first of several chapters addressing "Other Considerations."

Cheated On

Chapter 10
The Kids

> "So commit yourselves wholeheartedly to these words of mine…. Teach them to your children. Talk about them when you are at home and when you are on the road, when you are going to bed and when you are getting up."
> – Deuteronomy 11:18a, 19, NLT

When I went through my divorce, I did not have to consider all the complexities that come with having children with a cheater. We were a childless couple.

I consider having such a childless marriage with a cheater as a mercy from God. The divorce was hard enough without the pain of losing time with beloved sons or daughters.

This chapter is in the book because I realize many faithful spouses need a pastor responding to their needs as both faithful spouses and parents. They have to deal with the complexities of having children with a cheater.

Since I am not a lawyer or a social worker, I am going to limit my thoughts in this chapter to principles of moral instruction and how to handle disclosing information to your children about your marriage's ending.

The Golden Rule is a good place to start in a discussion about working with children who have a cheater for a parent:

How would you feel if you were learning decades later—for the first time—that your parents had divorced over dad's serial cheating but mom (or vice versa) decided to keep this secret from you?

I suspect your response would *not* be one of gratitude. Rather, it would be one of anger.

Personally, I imagine that I would feel doubly betrayed.

First, I would feel betrayed over my father's unfaithfulness to the family. Second, I would feel betrayed by my mother's unwillingness to give me this vital information that might have helped me to understand that confusing and traumatic time.

My suggestion is not to be the faithful parent who keeps such a nasty secret from your kids.

Followers of Christ are people who speak truth and not lies (e.g., John 3:19-21, Ephesians 4:25, etc.). And it is a lie of omission to keep this information from your children.

Tell the truth appropriately for their age.

You have an opportunity to teach basic morality to your child in this moment. They need to understand that adultery is not part of God's plan for marriage.

A six-year-old might only understand this lesson on the level of—say—"Daddy broke his promise to not have another 'girlfriend' than Mommy." But a teenager will understand much more as an almost-adult. Be sensitive to these differences, and do not insult the intelligence of your child.

That said, this is not about poisoning the child against the cheater by running the other parent down but rather being honest with the kids, respecting them enough not to lie. *Stick to the facts.* You do not have to editorialize with name-calling.

Telling the children will help them navigate this confusing time.

Life and healing come with truth. Destruction and death come with lies. These spiritual principles are especially applicable here.

Like a faithful spouse sensing the infidelity before having hard evidence, the children might have picked up this information or may have been made to carry the awful secret by the cheater. Either way, you are exposing darkness to light by naming the infidelity so that healing can take place.

Exposing the evil is what we are called to do as followers of Christ. The Apostle Paul says as much:

> "Take no part in the worthless deeds of evil and darkness; instead, expose them."
> – Ephesians 5:11, NLT

By letting your children know that unrepentant adultery is unacceptable in marriage, you are modeling godliness to them (see Jeremiah 3:8 and Matthew 1:19). Also, you are teaching them that actions have consequences.

They also can learn from your example not to tolerate infidelity and abuse in their future relationships.

I think that is a lesson worth having—a redemptive lesson even from the mess of evil that adultery is.

What about all the grief the parents hold? How ought a faithful spouse negotiate this grief while being a parent?

A classic mistake parents make with children when it comes to grief is to shield them from it. They do not let them go to the funeral of a beloved grandparent. And they do not cry in front of the kids.

This is not healthy.

Kids need to grieve the loss, too. They need to feel free to be sad and angry as well.

Cheated On

I say this as a professional chaplain who has extensive experience and expertise with grief. My advice to grieving parents:

Don't shutter your grief away as if it is something to be ashamed of. To do so is teaching your child to do the same.

That said, you do not want to make your child your emotional caregiver or direct your anger at them. *That is unhealthy.* The other extreme is to lie by denial about how you really feel about what really happened. *That is not healthy either.*

If asked, be honest. *Be real.*

When children see your tears, let them know those are sad tears as you feel sad over the marriage ending. People are often sad when they lose something that mattered to them. It is okay to be sad.

You are modeling the labeling of emotions as well as owning your own emotions to your child. They will see that having emotions—including sadness—is not a matter of shame.

This is another "teaching moment" opportunity that this difficult time offers you and your children.

You are equipping your child to go through his own emotional rollercoaster of grief without the added burden of shame that is too often the case in our grief-denying culture.

As a parent, we have opportunities to equip our children to negotiate this sin-broken world successfully. A divorce after adultery—while not a welcomed experience—does provide many teaching moments to help a faithful spouse bring up a child in godliness and health.

Take those opportunities to speak the truth in love. Let the child know what happened in an age-appropriate, factual way.

Next, take the opportunity to teach basic morality to your child. Let them understand adultery comes with consequences, and one of those is the ending of marriage in divorce. They need to understand this basic moral teaching regarding the seriousness of this sin.

Finally, you have an opportunity to teach your child how to grieve well. Instead of hiding the grief away, I encourage you to share factual statements about your emotions when asked.

Do not make your child the dumping ground of your emotions.

However, the child needs to understand from you that it is okay to feel the emotions of grief. They need to see shame-free grieving modeled for them.

In the next chapter in "Other Considerations," I tackle some gray areas regarding divorce. In particular, I share some of my thoughts on abandonment, abuse, and annulment.

Cheated On

Rev. David Derksen

Chapter 11
Abandonment, Abuse, And Annulment

> "But if the unbelieving spouse wants a divorce, then let it be so. In this situation the believing spouse is not bound to the marriage, for God has called us to live in peace."
> – 1 Corinthians 7:15, TPT

This book is written to help faithful spouses and their supporters dealing with adultery and divorce. But I also wanted to spend a chapter talking about other situations related to divorce and how I would apply the Bible pastorally to those situations.

Abandonment

A group often missed in the Christian discussion of adultery and divorce is that of faithful spouses abandoned by their adulterous ones. *I am in this group.*

I can tell you this experience comes with its own unique package of pain born from a heightened sense of powerlessness, rejection, and sometimes blame on top of that from the Christian community.

One of the most frustrating and painful aspects of the ecclesiastical trial I successfully negotiated was how the reality of being abandoned was practically ignored. It did not seem to matter who initiated the divorce. The questions were the same.

The trial—which for others may be a more informal trial of opinions—focused on the decision to divorce:

"Can you give me a biblical reason for your divorce?"

The problem with this was that they were trying the one left behind who did not make the decision to divorce. *Such questioning adds insult to a nasty, nasty injury—i.e., being abandoned.*

I felt like I was being held answerable for my former wife's sin—and divorcing me was sin in her case as an adulteress.

Maybe you can relate?

While I do not know what questions your family, friends, or church leaders have asked you about being abandoned, I can share the question that was used to cause me considerable suffering. It was a question echoed with slight variation by my former spouse and her family frequently in my ordeal. In fact, they attempted to get me to believe this was the most important question to ask myself about my disintegrating marriage:

"Why did she have to leave you?"

This question and its variations are the wrong sort of question to ask a faithful spouse after he or she has been abandoned. It encourages mind-reading and taking responsibility for a choice he or she did not make. As such, it is guaranteed to add to the trauma of abandonment and compound the already extreme emotional suffering of the faithful spouse.

The faithful spouse has just had their soul severed by the rejection of a spouse with whom they were formerly one. Blaming them for this trauma by asking this question is not going to aid in the healing process.

Furthermore, it is possible—as in my situation—that the question is based on a false premise. The question assumes the abandoning spouse *had to* abandon the relationship. This is an example of a fallacy in reasoning—a loaded question.

A classic example of this is the question: *When will you stop hitting your wife?* The question presumes the husband is hitting his wife. It is a no-win situation to answer it if he is not.

So, if you are like me and have experienced a variation on this question, I encourage you to reject Satan's lies. Speak the truth to yourself until you believe it:

> *"He did not have to leave. He chose to quit on us and leave."*
> *"I am not responsible for another person's choices and actions. I am only responsible for my own."*
> *"I do not know why she chose to leave; that is a question for her to answer. I cannot see into her heart."*

While this is a loaded question for some, it is not always the case. In some cases, a spouse might need to remove themselves from the marriage due, for example, to extreme physical abuse or other life-endangering behavior on the part of the other spouse. The next section in this chapter addresses these situations.

Abuse

Providing biblical perspective on divorce after abuse is a tricky subject. Domestic abuse is not a named subject within the Bible. However, I do believe some conclusions can be drawn from general principles in the Bible.

The big question I will address in this section is this:

> ## *Is domestic abuse grounds for a biblical divorce?*

Let's begin with something I believe is not in a gray area on this subject:

> ### *Domestic abuse is absolutely grounds for separation in order to protect the victim(s).*

However, the question under consideration here is not whether or not one is allowed to separate from an abuser. The question is whether a victim can biblically divorce his or her abuser.

80

Cheated On

Answering this question takes wisdom and discernment because the Bible does not address this matter explicitly. This is not an explicit exception under the godly divorce option for Christians.

However, I do see a possible way it fits with a well-established exception to the divorce prohibition.

To avoid overreliance on the Old Testament teachings and their rabbinical interpretations (which Jesus rejects in Matthew 19:1-12), we look to 1 Corinthians 7:15 for guidance that may apply to divorce in abuse situations.

> "But if the unbelieving spouse wants a divorce, then let it be so. In this situation the believing spouse is not bound *to the marriage*, for God has called us to live in peace."
> −1 Corinthians 7:15, TPT

This is the second grounds for divorce made explicit in the New Testament—namely, *the abandonment of an unbelieving spouse.* Most compassionate pastors would utilize this exception to deal with domestic abuse.

The reasoning is this:

1. Ongoing domestic abuse is an indication that the abuser is not a Christian (see Hebrews 10:26-27).
2. The separation caused by the abuse—for the safety of the victim—fulfills the physical abandonment part noted in the verse.

Obviously, as I mentioned earlier, I believe a separation in the case of domestic abuse is a *must!* Human life is precious to God as we are all made in His image. Separation ought to be taken to preserve life.

A healthy church leadership ought to aid a faithful spouse to deal with an abusive partner in these matters. This is the time for pastors and Christian leaders to encourage healthy steps to ensure safety for the faithful party and clear support to leave a relationship where safety is a concern.

Rev. David Derksen

The faithful spouse might decide to stay married. However, the pastor and Christian leaders ought to encourage the faithful party to not rush back into a dangerous situation without first ensuring a track record of change demonstrated by the abuser's actions and a safety plan in place. Repentance needs verification. Even if there is some signs of change, the wisest course may be divorce as the trauma wounds run deep.

Even saying that, I want to emphasize that this is an *interpretation* and *application of said interpretation* of Scripture. As I mentioned at the beginning, the Bible is not clear or explicit in these circumstances.

I may have this wrong. But if I am erring, I am erring on the side of mercy toward the innocent party here—i.e., the abuse survivor.

Still, it is important that the survivor only takes the step to divorce an abuser if she is convinced God is leading her to do so from her own reading of the Bible. Ultimately, it is the abuse survivor's decision to make. They have to live with its consequences (see 2 Corinthians 5:10).

I heartily recommend making such a decision about divorce with a few wise and seasoned Christian friends. Having the help of a healthy Christian community to discern these difficult matters is important and is part of the reason why we need to belong to a God-honoring church, in my opinion.

I am saddened by the need to provide the following caveat about abuse in marriages:

Is it really abuse or am I trying to get out of my commitment to a difficult relationship with communication issues? As one of my counselors once told me, "emotional abuse" means different things to different people.

Cheaters may use the "abuse" reasoning to retroactively justify leaving their faithful partner. They invent abuse charges about the faithful party to gain favor with counselors and pastors so that those Christian leaders do not pressure them to stay married (or stop cheating, even). Such a tactic is

Cheated On

easily dealt with by first requiring an explicit naming of the abuse and a call for repentance.

Without going through the full list of abuses, I would just point out faithful spouses often endure a wide variety of abuse on top of the infidelity. This would include financial abuse, emotional abuse, and spiritual abuse, to name just a few. Some cheaters are sly enough to keep their infidelity secret, but the abuse may be the "tell" regarding their hidden sinful life.

To be clear: *Any* form of abuse is completely unacceptable in a godly marriage!

In sum, I lean toward believing domestic abuse is grounds for biblical divorce based on 1 Corinthians 7:15. That said, this is *my interpretation.* Domestic abuse as grounds is not explicitly clear in the Bible. However, what is clear is that God does not want innocent blood shed (Proverbs 6:17) and that He cares for the vulnerable always (Psalm 82:3-4).

The next section is about as clear in the Scripture as the adultery exception for divorce. I will talk about what Scripture says about marriage annulment.

Annulment

Marriage annulment is related to divorce, but it is *very* different. They are not the same thing:

The big difference is that a divorce acknowledges a valid marriage existed, whereas an annulment says it was never a valid marriage.

Now, many will immediately think of the Roman Catholic Church when they hear the words, "marriage annulment." I am not talking about that process here.

For those unaware, Roman Catholics engage in a complicated process to determine the sacramental validity or invalidity of a marriage. They

83

have canonical law that guides this spiritual discernment process. An official marriage annulment from the Catholic Church is required for divorced Catholics if they want to remarry and remain in good standing with the Catholic Church.

Since I am a Protestant minister, I dare not dive into the intricacies of another faith group's theology and approach to marriage annulment. My expertise lies elsewhere.

So, in this section, I am talking about the garden-variety civil annulment of a marriage. This is the type where someone is withholding important information in order to get married, for example.

Does the Bible support such a civil annulment of a marriage?

While the Bible does not tackle this issue using that exact term, I think it does say something about the matter through the life of the Patriarchs. In particular, I think the Bible gives us a clear picture from the life of Abraham, who notoriously pushed his wife Sarah into fraudulent "marriages."

To Be Clear: I Am Firmly In The Camp Of "Yes, The Bible Supports Marriage Annulments."

Genesis 12:18-19 forms some of my biblical support for this position (also see Genesis 20).

> "But the Lord sent terrible plagues upon Pharaoh and his household because of Sarai, Abram's wife. So Pharaoh summoned Abram and accused him sharply. 'What have you done to me?' he demanded. 'Why didn't you tell me she was your wife? Why did you say, "She is my sister," and allow me to take her as my wife? Now then, here is your wife. Take her and get out of here!'"
> – Genesis 12:17-19, NLT

Clearly, God does not view a "marriage" as valid when one party is already married to another, as in the case of Sarai. He sent painful

Cheated On

judgment down upon Pharaoh for his—however unwitting—violation of Abram and Sarai's marriage.

From Abraham's poor example, I see a teaching in which fraudulent circumstances make ruling the marriage invalid acceptable for followers of Christ.

A modern example where annulment of a marriage applies as I see this is when marriage is used as a vehicle to obtain immigration status. The foreign spouse did not enter into the relationship in good faith. They withheld this important purpose—i.e., information—from their partner.

Another example where annulment is pertinent is when a spouse did not disclose prior to the nuptials that he or she would not have sex with their partner after marriage. This is important information needed prior to the marriage. Sexual relations are part of the marriage covenant unless otherwise agreed upon by both parties due to their circumstances.

Now some pastoral thoughts:

Fighting for these "marriages" makes as much sense as saying that God ought to have insisted Sarai stay with Pharaoh (or Abimelech in the Genesis 20 story). *This is an absurd stance to take.*

Furthermore, insisting on fighting for those subsequent "marriages" would entail denying that the existing marriage—in this case, Sarai's marriage to Abram—ever existed to begin with. In reality, she was ineligible to marry, and Pharaoh (plus Abimelech) reportedly would never have attempted to marry her if they had known she was already wed to Abram.

Refusal to accept marriage annulments may just be an extension of divorce prejudice applied to these situations.

In the effort to discourage divorce, pastors sometimes conflate categories by teaching annulment is the same thing as divorce. They end

Rev. David Derksen

up defending a position God never intended them to defend—i.e., fighting for nonexistent marriages.

Focusing on divorce as the problem as opposed to the moral consequence of one spouse's adulterous sin, it is easy to see how pastoral laziness can result in such an error. "Intact" marriages become an idol to be worshiped and served at all costs. That cost includes ignoring a biblical understanding of marriage annulment.

So, you find yourself divorced due to adultery, abandonment, or abuse. Or perhaps your marriage has been annulled. You now have to deal with false friends and your former in-laws. I address those dynamics in my next chapter in "Other Considerations."

Cheated On

Chapter 12
False Friends & Ex In-Laws

> "Do not plot harm against your neighbor, who lives trustfully near you."
> – Proverbs 3:29, NIV

As I covered in the beginning of this book, adultery is not a private matter. The sins involved in cheating ripple through a community.

This section is dedicated to negotiating the tricky waters of working with false friends and former in-laws. When we talk about grief, the loss of these relationships is also part of the massive losses that faithful spouses undergo with a cheating spouse.

What about friends during this period of cheating discovery and divorce? How do I discern who is a good and safe friend?

To answer that, we have to have a clear picture of what a true friend is and is not. Some might think the answer is obvious, but even the obvious is hard to grasp while dealing with the sucker-punch that adultery discovery is.

A true friend is someone who empathizes with you and does not condemn or label you.

I will never forget the words of a wise Catholic priest I spoke with in the aftermath of my divorce. We were discussing a judgmental "friend" who had labeled me. In reality, this "friend" had attacked me verbally. This priest said, "That does not sound like a friend to me."

It was obvious. However, I had never made the connection until that moment. The priest was correct. A friend does not attack and condemn another friend by calling them something derogatory. They do not use shame as a weapon to harm a friend whom they genuinely love.

Another sign of a true friend is that this person recognizes the friendship is a gift and treats access to your heart as such. They do not act as if they are entitled to speak into your life without consequence.

A true friend may speak a difficult or hard word, but they do so with love and kindness, respecting the autonomy of their friend to listen to this word or not. They are willing to accept that this hard word may not be well received by their friend in the moment and they will not hold that reaction against them.

Such a good friend might call out a spouse who is being naïve about their partner's activities. They might warn them such behavior is consistent with cheating and encourage their friend to get tested for STDs. That is a hard word, but it may literally be life-saving.

Another hard word from a friend may be simply a reminder about what the faithful spouse controls—i.e., himself or herself. They might deliver the awful reminder that a cheater can leave and the abandoned spouse does not control the situation. That is a tough word but often necessary to refocus the faithful party on what he or she DOES control in these situations—i.e., their own decisions and actions.

In contrast, a false friend believes he gets to tell you what to do, and you *must* obey him.

He acts entitled to know everything about you *because he is a Christian "brother."* This person is not in the relationship to serve you but to serve himself. Beware of this wolf in sheep's fleece.

Another sign of a true friend is they genuinely care about the trauma you endured and refuse to remain neutral about your soul rape. This is very important to remember when sorting through your "friends" list post-infidelity discovery.

Use "The Soul Rape Test" on your friendships:

Imagine you informed a friend that a mutual friend sexually assaulted you. Your assailant admits to it. What happened is not a matter for debate. It occurred.

A true friend does not show callous indifference to this information. They do not try to excuse the perpetrator of such evil and ask you what you did to "make them" harm you in this way. The true and godly friend does not seek to maintain neutrality on the matter.

A true friend stands firmly and unequivocally with the victim. They are horrified and saddened their friend was abused in such a wicked and treacherous way!

If a friend responds otherwise to your revelation of the marital infidelity, you will know them as a false friend. Friends do not act neutral when their true friend has had their soul raped.

Now, once you know whether a friend is true, you are equipped to let the relationship go or cultivate it further. Life is too short to allow people access to your heart who are not true and godly friends. You do not need further treachery.

What about ex in-laws?

Your in-laws are in a very difficult position. They may feel great shame over the behavior of their child. If there is history of marital infidelity in their family—or even possibly in their own marriage—the pain and shame might be too much for them to confront in a godly way.

Another complicating factor for former in-laws is if grandchildren are part of the picture. They might fear losing contact and relationship with those precious grandchildren if they are too hard on their own child.

Do not underestimate the power of biology in these situations. Most will be biologically inclined to take the side of their cheating son or daughter. It is hard to swallow the reality that your child did something as bad as violating their marriage vows by committing adultery.

Some in-laws will rise above this biological disposition to stand on the path of righteousness. They will refuse to engage in some version of The Shared Responsibility Lie.

Cheated On

Instead, godly ex in-laws will condemn the behavior of their child as wrong while understanding such condemnation does *not* mean they have to stop loving said child. In fact, I would argue such condemnation is the sign of true love as it means the in-laws understand the spiritual peril for their child's soul (see Hebrews 10:26-27). They understand their child's spiritual well-being depends upon that child repenting of their sins.

If you are blessed to have such godly ex in-laws, please thank them, and if applicable, allay their fears about losing contact with the grandchildren. They are being courageous in taking such a moral stand. Do not take their support for granted. Not every faithful spouse is so fortunate as to have godly ex in-laws.

What if you do not have godly in-laws?

I would say to treat them like you would a false friend. Keep them at a distance as they are no good for you. Do not allow them to mess with your head about your now-defunct marriage. Choose not to listen to their ungodly noise.

They can believe and say whatever they like. However, you are free to believe the spiritual reality that the only path to spiritual life is the path of repentance for their child.

This leads me to my final point in this chapter:

To heal from infidelity, a faithful spouse must learn to let go of the compulsion to get narrative agreement.

Cheaters will likely say all sort of awful things about you and the marriage. They will likely present a retroactive, negative marriage narrative in order to address their guilt over blowing up the marriage with their infidelity.

You have power in this. Do not give it back to the cheater or lousy in-laws!

The power you have is in writing and believing your own story. You do not have to have their agreement to know and believe the truth. Let them live in their reality of distorting lies. You do not need their agreement with the truth to live in it.

I realize this is easier said than done. If you did not care about the person's opinion, you probably would not have married them or allowed them to become your friend in the first place.

However, your healing from this trauma requires letting go of relationships that suck you back into lies and reality distortions. *You must let them go.* The cost of their agreement is too high.

Find true friends who care about the truth and godliness!

Now that you have some tools to deal with false friends and your former in-laws, I turn to share some final wisdom about emotional affairs in the last chapter of "Other Considerations."

Cheated On

Chapter 13
Is It Really "Just" An Emotional Affair?

> "You have heard that it was said, 'You shall not commit adultery.' But I tell you that anyone who looks at a woman lustfully has already committed adultery with her in his heart."
> – Matthew 5:27-28, NIV
> "But among you there **must not be even a hint of sexual immorality,** or of any kind of impurity, or of greed, because these are improper for God's holy people."
> – Ephesians 5:3, NIV (emphasis added)

With adultery being the clearest example that grant a faithful spouse grounds for a biblical divorce (see Deuteronomy 22:22, Jeremiah 3:8, and Matthew 19:9), this inevitably leads to the question of what to do with an admitted emotional affair.

It did not involve sexual contact with another person. *So, does an emotional affair matter in God's eyes?*

Yes, it does matter, and greatly.

Emotional affairs are not acceptable in God's eyes. Jesus' own words suggest He recognized that emotional affairs or affairs in the heart are serious. He did not give them a pass in the Sermon on the Mount.

Jesus condemns emotional affairs. *So, how ought we to handle emotional affairs when disclosed to us as pastors or Christian leaders?*

Cheated On

I will utilize a fictitious case study to talk about addressing emotional affairs from my own perspective. Here's a scenario:

> *A wife comes into the pastor's office with her husband. Both are professing Christians and members of the church. The wife produces risqué electronic messages between her husband and another woman. Her husband admits to having an emotional affair, but he claims that was "all." He then launches into a story about how he felt neglected at home and just fell prey to this flirtatious woman from work. That's why he had an emotional affair. He never would have had an emotional affair if his wife had been better at loving and respecting him at home.*

1. First, I would encourage the pastor to reflect back what was admitted and thereby confront the unfaithful spouse with his sin.

It is important to protect the faithful spouse. She has just experienced a wicked sucker-punch from her trusted spouse. It is traumatic and disorienting, to say the least!

The pastor is not directly involved in the marriage and is in a position of power that can help. Be strong and do not minimize this sin.

Take this admission of an emotional affair or adultery of the heart very seriously, just as Jesus does in the Sermon on the Mount (Matthew 5:27-28). Do not accept blame-shifting from the cheating spouse. This helps no one and harms both spouses spiritually as it is a false teaching. *One is only responsible for one's own sin and not another's (see 2 Corinthians 5:10).*

Here's a suggested model response to the unfaithful husband:

> *"I just heard you admit to violating your marriage vows by having an emotional affair. Your wife did not sin by having an affair. You did. "For the sake of your marriage and your soul, I suggest you stop blaming other people for your own sinful choices and actions. Repentance cannot even begin until you own your sin fully and stop blaming your wife or the marriage conditions."*

Rev. David Derksen

2. Don't be naïve: Liars lie.

> *Just because he said he did not have sex with the other woman does not make it so!*

It is dangerously naïve and foolish to trust an admitted liar's words at face value. You have discovered this individual was engaged in deception in order to maintain an emotional affair. I would suggest that you *assume* it went further than what the cheater admitted.

I feel taking this default stance of guilt after an admission or evidence of an emotional affair is important on two levels:

1. *Defaulting to assuming a sexual affair is a wise stance to take when dealing with a known liar.* Their words cannot be trusted.
2. *Defaulting to assuming a sexual affair leaves biblical divorce on the table for the faithful spouse without a hint of condemnation.* The faithful spouse may never be able to prove her spouse had sex with the other woman. However, she has proof her husband violated the marriage covenant by having an emotional affair, at minimum.

To be clear:

I am not saying that a faithful spouse should necessarily divorce over an emotional affair alone.

However, I *am* saying divorce may be the best of the bad options in some circumstances involving an emotional affair.

I am encouraging outsiders—especially pastors—to keep a clear head and not get sucked into the deception that it was "only" an emotional affair because the cheater said so. Don't let your desire as a pastor or Christian leader to salvage the marriage blind you to the obvious (e.g., he had many opportunities to commit adultery and a desire to do so).

Cheated On

I say trusting the cheating spouse's word is a *dangerous* mistake to make because it may involve leaving the faithful spouse open to getting an STD.

Would you want to risk your own life on the word of a proven liar? I wouldn't.

As a basic act of good faith, I would suggest asking the cheating spouse to get tested. If pushback occurs, point out that he broke his wife's trust by having an emotional affair, and it is reasonable to ask him to give her concrete proof she is minimally safe from STDs. It ought to be no big deal getting tested if he actually cares about his wife (and is not lying).

3. Be aware: Strong incentives exist to NOT admit to sexual sin in evangelical Christian circles.

The Bible's teaching on emotional affairs is just not as clear and direct as its teachings on adultery. This creates wiggle room for the unfaithful spouse if he only admits to an emotional affair.

If successful in confessing and blame-shifting, he might even be able to walk out of the pastor's office after spending the lion's share of the time talking about his *wife's* "deficiencies" as opposed to his adultery of the heart. This becomes much more difficult to accomplish if he admits to adultery.

Evangelicals generally take sexual sin more seriously than other sin (at least, that is my experience). By confessing adultery, the cheating spouse is "giving" his Christian wife a clear, biblical way out of the marriage. She can divorce him (Matthew 19:9), and he would look *really* bad to other Christians who found out why.

In short, the power would shift drastically away from the cheating "Christian" spouse if he admitted to more than an emotional affair. All these things are strong reasons *to lie!*

In closing, I offer these thoughts as counsel I *wished* a pastor in my life had followed when I had clear evidence of an emotional affair, which

Rev. David Derksen

came before the clear evidence of adultery. As pastors and Christian leaders, we need to grow in street wisdom on these matters.

> "Look, I am sending you out as sheep among wolves. So be as shrewd as snakes and harmless as doves."
> – Matthew 10:16, NLT

We need to understand the biblical texts applicable to emotional affairs and come at these situations with open eyes to the depravity of human behavior. Ignorance in either department is a recipe for disaster.

Cheated On

Conclusion
Testifying To Real Hope

> "Forget the former things; do not dwell on the past. See, I am doing a new thing! Now it springs up; do you not perceive it? I am making a way in the wilderness and streams in the wasteland."
> – Isaiah 43:18-19, NIV

When adultery is discovered, the faithful spouse is understandably thrown into a dark place—a wasteland. This book is primarily about addressing and surviving that wasteland.

But the story of the wasteland is only a chapter or footnote to the testimony God is writing with the faithful spouse's life. It *is* a wasteland.

But…our God is the Creator who sends streams into wastelands, transforming them into luscious gardens of joy.

My encouragement to other faithful spouses is to go out and discover the destiny or works God prepared in advance for you to do.

> "Even before we were born, God planned in advance *our destiny* and the good works we would do *to fulfill it!*"
> – Ephesians 2:10b, TPT

The marital infidelity, abandonment, and divorce are simply part of our life story. We *are* victims of our former spouse's sins against us. However, we are *more than* victims. We are faithful spouses with works to do for God.

Christ's Bride, the Church, needs us.

It may not feel that way. You may feel like you are a second-class citizen because of your divorce. That is not how God sees it, though.

Cheated On

You have survived a fire of testing most Christians—thankfully—never will endure. And you came out as a faithful spouse. Your character is fire-proven gold!

Plus, you now have a testimony to share. This testimony has power.

Who knows? Maybe your testimony will be what helps a despairing and demonically assailed faithful spouse choose life over death.

> "For the accuser of our brothers and sisters, who accuses them before our God day and night, has been hurled down. They triumphed over him by the blood of the Lamb and by the word of their testimony..."
> – Revelation 12:10b-11a, NIV

Each of our destinies looks different. For some, that new life will include a new spouse and family. For others, it might include a new career or new hobbies—or a new ministry.

This may be the first time you are set free to become the unique and wonderful human God made you to be!

Explore your likes and try new things. Remember that God values you so much that He shed the most precious of substances, His Son's blood. Go on an adventure of discovery with the One who is madly in love with you!

Rev. David Derksen

Cheated On

Rev. David Derksen

About The Author

Reverend David Derksen is a Board Certified Chaplain (BCC), ordained minister, and graduate of Yale Divinity School. His blog *"Divorce Minister: Taking Adultery Seriously"* won first listing on Feedspot's 2018 "Top 10 Christian Divorce Blogs and Websites On the Web." Pastor David lives in the state of Minnesota where he is very happily remarried and a father.

Made in the USA
Monee, IL
06 July 2023